Orrin Cedesman Stevens

An Idyl of the Sun

And Other Poems

Orrin Cedesman Stevens

An Idyl of the Sun
And Other Poems

ISBN/EAN: 9783744704793

Printed in Europe, USA, Canada, Australia, Japan

Cover: Foto ©Thomas Meinert / pixelio.de

More available books at **www.hansebooks.com**

An Idyl of the Sun

AND

Other Poems.

BY

Orrin Cedesman Stevens.

HOLYOKE, MASS.
Griffith, Axtell & Cady Company.
1891

CONTENTS.

An Idyl of the Sun

and

Other Poems.

ERRATA.

Page 46, line 2, for *reflection* read *refection*.

Page 73, line 6, for *besides* read *beside*.

Page 98, line 8, for *disorded* read *disordered*.

Page 105, line 15, for *has* read *hast*.

AN IDYL OF THE SUN.

ARDO. Above the white crown of our sacred tree,
Whose roots are watered by the seven streams
Which issue from one fount, let us retire ;
And let the radiance of its luminous leaves,
Which furnish light to earth, afford us shade.
And we will leave unaided, for awhile,
Our dear companions of the forceful rites,
And mingle new with simpler, ancient joys.—
See ! as I kiss thy loving lips again,
That new, red rose hang quivering on its stalk,
Before the window of that far earth home.
TINTA. And I will think of thee, and breathe thy name,
To give it deeper fragrance.
ARDO.   I will take thy hand
In mine, and hold it long and restfully,
To make the flower cling firmly to its stem,
Until some lover asks it as a mate
To his beloved's heart.
TINTA.   I give thee thanks,
O lover, husband, prince, that thou dost yet
Give thought to me, and still the joy dost find,

Which thou didst put into my heart on earth.
For when I see those seven chromatic bands—
The symbols of the seven solar powers—
So clear upon thy radiant white arm,
And then look down upon mine own, to find
One only shining dimly in its place,
I sorrow inconsolably ; and would
That all the glories which beset mine eyes
Were changed for store of common, earthly tears,
Which may not be found here. Still dost thou stoop,
As ever thou hast done, to give me love.
ARDO. Tinta, there is no high or low to hearts !
They ever rock upon the same sea-level,
Feel the same tides, and in the frequent calms,
Moor their light keels with rapture side by side.
Speak not of tears ; in all this wizard world
There is no craftsman who can make a tear !
Nor in the universe, might there be found
Essence so fine, hue so immaculate
(Not even if we sought amid the dreams
And vision-daring purposes of gods)
As might be moulded into fitting tears
For thy pure eyes. Think nevermore of grief !
Grief is a cripple who can never move,
Save when supported by two subject hearts,
One on each side. Ah, sweet, apostate soul,
One cannot mourn without another's aid ;
And I alone might aid thee and I will not.

Again I say, I love thee ! be thou glad !
TINTA.   Oh, that word love, when spoken by thy lips,
Doth shape itself into a trumpet's curves,
Through which the voice of some far deity
Doth storm the last earth rampart of my heart,
And take it prisoner to a deathless thrall !
Now, *first* I look upon thee without fear,
Since thou didst shore for me, with thine own breast,
The boundless stream which bore me hitherward ;
Whereon the earth danced like a withered leaf,
And all the stars seemed whirling molecules
Of phosphorescent frenzy.   Now, I dare
To note how thou art changed : how thy new life
Seems like a crystal sheath upon the old,
Hiding no loving line, but adding to it.
It is as though thine older, lesser form,
Compressed by muscle bands, which grooved the arms,
Girt close the struggling waist, and tightened down
The mighty shoulders' buoyancy,
Had lightly, when the corded thongs were cut,
By force of its divine, expansive energy,
Sprung up to its balked stature, and revealed
Its natural majesty all unrestrained.
As now I gaze, thy broad, bright bosom seems
A golden stream, deep in whose lighted depths,
Are imaged clearly all the godlike deeds
And tender favors of o'erhanging arms,
With shadowy, dim shapes associate,

Of future fondness brooding in thy heart.
Upon its peaceful currents are mine eyes
Borne on, with wonder, to the whirlpool face,
Which draws mine own into its blissful charm.
Here, in a spirit trance, I travel round and round,
Tapering the large delight down to a point,
That I may ever again look away.
O speech divine ! that, like a cleansing storm,
Doth sweep from seraph lips all vestiges
Of faulty human uses, and leaves bare
The prints of love alone.   Thy lips are changed.
Yet are the likeness of the lips I kissed
With freedom on the earth.   So sentient
In every point thy light-absorbing face,
Vision doth never weary thy calm eyes,
But leaves them fresh for forming loving looks :
Else might I never look upon thee thus.
ARDO.   Remembrest thou, dear Tinta, how, on earth,
A little thing grew larger when advanced
Close to the eyes? and canst thou now believe
That, the vast spaces of material things
Dispelled between us, and thy very self
Brought near my spiritual vision, there is room
For my glad sight to pass thy broadened beauty?
Nay then ! it stops in thee, and is filled up,
Contented, to its farthest boundaries !
Thinkest thou that the diver finds the pearl
As lovely in its shady place, as when

The sun shall dry the moistened gem in his hand,
Above the water? Shall not the obscure,
But matchless fabrics of night's labratories,
When set in morning's open galleries,
Extract new wonder from our stricken sight?
O thou who wert the fairest thing on earth !
By bathing in our iridescent streams,
Thou hast imparted to thy gathered grace
The mermaid's dripping beauty. Scarce I dare
To look upon one place, so dangerous
Its violent splendor to my careless eyes,
Relaxed and resting ; but, secure, I turn
Them to thine own, which lie like peaceful isles,
Twinned in a sea of glory, and now stilled
By the soft wavelets of thy soothing lids
To an enchanted peace. How vast the space
From those young worlds to the old grizzled earth
Toward which they turn !
Tinta.   My wonder cannot cease,
When I look down upon the earth, and see
How changed she seems. See now, how dull she is !
As she doth blindly stagger on between
Those close and cousinly divinities, ˙
Twilight and Dawn. How earnestly they strive
To rouse the memories of an earlier life
Of star-like energy ! See, how the wind
Doth beat her heavy temples, and the scourge
Of lightning's passion strikes her senseless back !

Even the sleeping Titan in her heart
Starts vainly in her dreams, and fitfully
Doth struggle, though unconscious! But, alas!
The stupor lingers. Now she dumbly turns,
Until the sunrise warms the very spot
Where we first loved. There *must* be feeling *there*!
ARDO. O sunrise of the earth, what is thy pain!
How dost thou mourn for all that thou dost miss,
Each morning, from the open treasuries
Heaped by the last day's potent industry!
What traveler of the shining, silvery road
Of life and love, when he falls headlong down
The frequent chasms dug by Night and Sleep,
Drops nothing from his bruised and aching hand?
O how may one fit on the broken stalk
Of yesterday, new flowers of this day's happiness?
How may his span of love reach far as that of life,
When darkness hinders not the one, but coils
The other back upon weak memories?
Ever, on earth, is day's love-ripened fruit
Pecked by the Vulture Night!
TINTA   But one who loves,
Will sleep so light, and keep her heart so white,
That no night birds shall find there any perch;
And day shall add itself to day, and love
Stretch far and flawless.
ARDO.   Yes, when that one be as thou.
But yet, how blind and weak we were, at best!

How hidden from ourselves our spiritualities !
And how we aided our own hindrances !
Often, when thou didst offer me, with smiles,
Thy right hand's treasures, I would seize the left ;
Or when the very symbol of thy soul
Sat on thy silent lips, mine own have broke
The holy thing with missile words ; and when
Thy solar-working heart built round mine own
Halos to bless it, I have broken through.
Oft in the white flower of thy love I saw
Only the earth honey ; from thy purest word,
Have turned to kiss the lip's red stain, and thus
Defrauded thy sweet heart.   And many times
Those star songs that do sound alone through lips
Of fortunate moments, have been fiercely scorned,
For those coarse strains, which only may be struck
From strings of sensuous days.
TINTA.   But, even then
Thou lovedst me as now ; 'twas ever plain :
Error's tortuous path led ever to that goal.
The widening circles in the troubled deeps
Sprung from a golden stone.   Pain cold not pluck
The one white feather from her raven wings ;
And every horrifying thing was wreathed
With visions of thy name.   And many times
The iron ball of inconsiderate speech,
By the swift fervor of love's afterthought,
Was melted ere it struck ; while, frequently,

I wronged thee with mistaken estimates
Of thine own worth. That mighty will of thine
Seemed often but the body's urgency,
The downward plunging of the waterfall,
Instead of the strong geyser's living leap :
Yet would I see the rainbow of thy love
Upon it, and feared not.

ARDO.   Still blind were we,
And blind remain our fellows of the earth.
Yet naught gropes there but man : the flying cloud
Keeps well its path at midnight ; the lithe stream
Makes its long practiced leap from rock to rock,
When darkness drapes with doubt the changing way,
As surely as when sunlight leads : each flower
Finds its own place upon the populous stalk,
And fills the secret channels of the air
With flowing fragrance ; and the whole earth's
Dense barriers turn not the emerald streams,
Which hasten to the fountains of the trees :
But man must tremblingly and in the dark
Contest his spiritual footings ; be content
To touch, with blind and baffled finger-tips,
Only some earthly thing his spirit-mate
Has worn upon her heart : to wander round
And round the shrine wherein she lonely kneels
But find no entrance door on any side :
Nor hear the name of that divinity
She worships daily in her whispered prayer.

His senses seem but sheaths of some divine
And vibrant energies : like promontories,
Which jut into the deeps of the divine,
Are the vast cloud-heaps o'er his stormy thought,
Wherein his spirit-voice is faintly heard,
Like muffled thunders vaguely terrible :—
The cold, clay handles of the infinite,
Alone meet everywhere his own clay hand !
TINTA. But love, the subtle, incondensable,
Doth flow about him, like an atmosphere :
And golden-wingèd birds fly evermore
From soul to soul, with mystic messages
Not wholly written in unmeaning signs.
O husband of the two-fold unity !
Had I not learned, while yet upon the earth,
The outline of thine inner worthiness
And guessed the beauty of thy spirit face,
Could I have traced thee here ? But when lone Death,
With strange inversion of official power,
Did come and kill the whole material world,
To make thee live the plainer in my heart :
Saw I not there the very image of thyself?—
Thy luminous face turned hither, and thy hand
Stretched backward after mine ? And when I walked
Across the earthly ruin Death had made,
And followed thee in space, no need to ask :
"Where went the spirit stronger than the earth,
With solar flight and backward turning face?"

No need to seek the signal plumes let fall
From thy flame wings along the unknown way !
Thy distant goal I knew before I died ;
And I but turned my longing eyes that way,
And, on the currents of etherial life,
Did simply float again into thine arms.

    ARDO.   O sweetest drift that ever comforted
Those awful tides !   Wonder of woman's love !
That it had power to guide thee safely here,
And charm the deeps to render up their charge,
While still such rayless voids delay their currents,
Such drear, dead spaces !   Oh ! for this one hour,
Would I live myriads of darkened years
Upon the earth, in caverns unexplored
By all save Night, and where the baffled sight
Withers away in her black floating sand ;
Or be enclosed in countless folds of rock,
Bent for the purpose : or be ages whirled
Upon the trackless, unprogressing wheel
Of some air vortex !   Bright were that deep cave,
Where I might tunnel through the stagnant years
To find thy light !   Unfeared the rocky cell
Which opened at thy feet !   And there were peace
Within the whirlpool, if the last revolve
Should draw thee in !

                It is a grace unmatched
In all Infinity's love-laborings,
That our superior rites are not allowed to *one* ;

That only two, whose equal heart-beats strike
At the same moment, and evoke a sound
From out the slender scepter of our King,
Like his own holy music, can perform
Those ministrations nearest to his throne.
But thy true heart doth part its longing beat,
Beneath its polished silver bells, to catch
The single sound of mine between
Its clasping chimes, and keep it sweetly-safe,
In happy unison. I offer thanks !
That one alone dares not the highest joys ;
But two together, with their arms entwined,
And fingers clasped to brace the fragile heart,
Can only venture them, and cautiously.
"Tis said that there are orbs that restless roam
Through alien and unrecognizing worlds,
Inhabited by single, self-enveloped souls,
Who ever lie amid the fields' cold blanks,
Beneath a starless wreck of low, grey sky,
And contemplate their mighty, passive limbs,
Their useless arms, and breasts untenanted,
And hear the lone heart beat its solemn knell
Upon the trembling ground ; and they are bound
To stay in that eternal solitude ;
For they are powerless to summon there
Even a spectral life of phantasy
To share that boundless emptiness.
And when, sometimes, despairing they would thrust

The naked blade of vision, yet unfleshed
In the warm body of material things,
Back to its scabbard of the inner life,
They stop, appalled, before that awful view
Of darkened ruins, like a dead star's face,
Of rayless peaks and chasms probeless, black,
And mists of misery enshrouding all.
O I am glad that I may ever live,
Where many spirits, in the neighboring space,
Pass my weak thought along from point to point,
And speed its travels to the unseen God !—
May linger in the midst of this abounding life,
Which crowds the sky up to its noblest arch,
And bids it call upon the watchful stars
To closer stand, and cross their upright spears,
Lest something should escape their care.
TINTA.　O Ardo, as thou spokest of those souls
So far from God, because they are alone,
It seemed as though some smallest stalk of fear,
Long withered in the heart, had suddenly
Shot forth a shivering, black flower, that cast
A shadow on its open fount of peace.
O let me lay my head upon thy breast
That I may not forget thee for the length
Of one brief moment !　Now I feel secure,
And can again commune unfrighted with thee.
　When from this dear and sovereign seat of vision,
All visible things seem subject to my sight,

I am not chiefly glad that I can look
So far away through this transparent air,
And 'cross these shimmering fields of rainbow-harvests,
Where flowers seem only as expanded gems
With stems of lengthened pearl : that I can see
Unto the farthest verge of this sphere opulent,
Whereon, mayhap, some busy sister stands
And dips her ever dripping cup of flexile gold
Into the nearest spring, to quench the thirst
Of some exhausted pilgrim from a world
Whose founts are slowly failing ; nor, in sooth,
That my strong sight flies on beyond all spheres
Like this, to where a world lies spread—
As I may guess by those broad, wondrous rays
Which match the mountain peaks upon our own—
So bright, so limitless, that all these orbs
Which form our luminous community,
Are but dim tapers at her massive gates ;
Nor is this sight most dear, that it will go
Down and still down—so far, the falling stars
Have never reached the place—and dimly trace
The shadowy boundaries of those orbless souls,
Whose being is so large, so unrestrained,
That their least deed is vaster than our sun,
And no world yet is builded strong enough
To bear the beating of their strenuous hearts,
Or broad enough to make a worthy stage
For their exploits : but mostly give I praise,

That, whether thy heart turns in my love's breezes,
Or the pure juices of my sun-life's passion
Fall in the chalice of thy waiting wish,
Or miss it, I do see and know the *truth*.
And if thy spirit dons its shield of reverent awe,
And turneth inward to the seven Powers
That lie, concentric, round the fiery globe
Wherein our nameless and invisible King
Dwells in his long creative loneliness,
I know, and cease to babble of the things
Which make the gladness of our outward life.
ARDO.   Wondrous clairvoyancy of woman's love !
And chief of wonders, that such regal gift
Should be indentured to a single heart,
And that heart mine !   Oh, my clear eyes,
That seemed up-rounded on the earth, to let
The fairest things slip off them unobserved,
And now impression of supernal lives
Take from all sides !—though they may plainly see
How Heat and Light are wedded in one ray,
To be the sun's resplendent almoners ;
May see the indraft of that unillumined dust
Attrition's tribute from those ravaged worlds
Where that fair twain has been again divorced—
Though I may look far through our several plains
Of life down to that glowing, central sphere
Which is our sovereign's home, and see thereon
Bright flashes of imperfect images,

Fire hints and burning, fleeting flush of shades—
As if the god within, had, in a careless hour,
Thought fitfully of himself, and jeopardized
The awful secret of his shrouded life—
Yet how thy love is interblent with mine,—
That see I not. The mystic tie was wrought
Ere light was given to this shuttle heart,
Or by the artificer's shading hand
Was cunningly concealed. But if to-day
Thy love hath such a power, what will it be
When it may work in all the seven hues?
Now, as I speak, thy loving thought doth print
Upon the subtle substance of this air—
So sensitive to lovers—all the host
Of upstored graces fully perfected,
And filmy marvels of inceptive art :
So that I seem the only citizen
Of Love's etherial, blissful capital,
Built by benignant spell upon the peaks
Of highest moments buoyed aloft by joy :
But lest I lose my way in those bright streets.
Do thou unmake them by a gentle thought
Alien to ARDO. Wherefore tell me now,
What thou wilt do the rest of this long day
To further train thy finely-working hand?
TINTA. First, will I take a stealthy, potent charm
Unto a heart upon the earth unloved,
That it shall so bewilder, daze and draw

Some random love-prospector, haply near,
That he shall see the flitting, coaxing shapes
Which I commingle with its diamond deeps.
And, after, I will let selected rays
Pass freely through my open, love-clear heart,
And with accretion of resistless fire,
Burn into nothingness the barriers
Between attracted souls.   And what wilt thou?
ARDO.   I will instruct Desire to circle round thy head,
To take his course from thine own gentle thought,
And wing an even flight with its white plumes :
And I will strive to-day and every day,
To so discumber mine own heavy life
Of every stain of guilt or selfish thought,
And so assist my brothers at like work,
That this light-loaded orb may lightly vault
Into a higher place, and joyously
Expand, unhindered, to a nobler curve,
And make more room for seraphs ; constantly
Will I look through the armories of the sun,
Confer with foremost brethren, closely search
Our luminous archives' every crowded leaf,
And down into the dimmest places of the heart
Urge on the quest—study the faintest signs :
Yea, I will even waken Prophecy !
To learn the secret of a larger ray,
By which our gifts might grow to greater size.
TISLA.   Then, husband, we will ever join our hands

To fashion every gift ; thou shalt bestow
Its central core and amplitude of form,
And I will borrow of my purest joy,
To add the outward beauty. But, awhile,
Let us still tarry here ; soon, very soon,
The double yolk of this seclusion's shell
Shall alter to the broad, unresting wings
Of common life ; and while I keep my head
A little longer on this breast still mine,
Tell me the story thou hast promised oft
To tell me when my heart was well prepared.
ARDO. As thou desirest ; listen :   Long years ago,
Before the oldest ministrant now here
Had his bright birth upon some distant world,
'Tis said a splendid apparition streamed
Into our lightning-vaporous atmosphere,
Still shining with puisant light undimmed
When very near.   It was a spirit born
On that far orb incontinent of light,
Whose fullness overflows in circling bands
Of flaming energy, which make it seem
A prison-star built round with walls of fire.
His name was Vivero—for it is still preserved
Behind the prison bars of whitest lips
Whose whispered utterance seems its very ghost —
And as he clove his way with slow, spent wings
And face that reeked with toil of his long flight—
'Twas but a passing, starry mist upon it—

The startled watchers from their airy heights
Forgot their office, could but gaze in awe,
As did the whole sun people silently.
No being of such mien, none clad as he,
Had ever come before unto the sun ;
His stature equalled easily the height
Of that strange pillar of translucent gold
Some earlier race did build upon our sphere,
Which we have seen at sunrise from the earth :
His wings spread out like islands of the sea,
Pulsed by the sea into a crimson flush :
No shadow-moth had ever found a perch
Upon his radiant face, which blinding shone,
As if the light, o'erflowing from the eyes,
Suffused it with a glamor of the grace
Which we are taught to gather in the soul
For inner vision ; downward from the chin,
The mighty veins of his unhindered neck
Were sluices round of lightning-driven fire ;
And all the vast recumbence of his form
Seemed like a valley plucked from paradise,
With all its mighty, silver tentacles
Still clinging to its undismembered mass,
And million-tinted herbage undisturbed.

As near he came the poison-stricken air,
Which till that day had been a moteless sheen,
Writhed with convulsions of a mother's pangs,
Brought forth from quick gestations unperceived

Her mistimed, unimagined progeny :
And storms did ravage all the solar world,
Tearing away from its immortal mines,
And from its altar-flames and subtle flowers,
And from the faces of the seraph saints,
A drift of shining dust, which floated long
Above the land.

      And when the sun's first floor
Bended beneath that alien angel's foot,
A faintness fell upon its countless founts,—
A dimness on its ever-living lights.
Our provinces upon the distant earth
And other planetary worlds adjoined—
Which now, with broad bands centrally enclasped,
Showeth their easy bondage—by degrees,
Surrendered their vast territories
Unto the white autochthons of the poles—
Ever in wait to seize their ancient lands—
Because their far and shining capital
Suffered a strange oppression, felt the first
Abasement of an evil spirit's light.

      Gracious and kind were Vivero's salutes :
Our people soon were cheated of their fears,
And did admit him to their sacred rites
And simple fellowship, if that be such,
Where Truth doth burn her veil and Error wears
Its ravished wraith.

      Infected time passed on :

The lofty Vivero had, one by one,
Acquired the use of all the seven Powers,
And bore the circling emblem on his arm.
Proudly, but vaguely, spoke he of the past,
Of Titan strifes and angel heroisms :
But from the fatal fabric of his speech,
His spell-instructed listeners ever built
Visions of stars despoiled and temples sacked,
Of shadowy forms dislimbed and spheres unrolled
In plains of even, uninspired light.
To break the weak delusion that a God
Lived in their secret cores.   But, day by day,
Did Vivero's heaven-challenging desire
Draw him still inward towards the flawless home
Of our benignant Lord : until, at last,
He passed beyond the farthest boundary
Of reverent life, and stood unharmed and proud
Within the regions of bold blasphemy.
Behind, the horror of the watching hosts
Closed like a parted wave : before him shone
The star of stars unchanged : onward he went,
Until the lengthened silence, which is night
Upon the sun, began : but still advanced
That strong adventurer.   The new day came,
But slow and feebly, as 'twere stricken old,
And could not bear the daring enterprise
Devolved upon it : low the waters sank
In all the springs : the currents of the streams

Ceased flowing, and the soulful flowers strewn
Upon their banks, down to the water's edge
Drooped plaintively ; and all the sun race moved
With languid steps and sad abasèd head,
As though their strength was gone, and hope beside.

   Still watching towards the close of that wan day
With desecrated eyes and stilled hearts,
They saw that arch-intruder pause, and turn
One moment towards them with a scornful smile.
Then spread his glorious wings and raise his hands
That were enfeoffed with sinful sovereignty,
And, like a wingèd avalanche in air,
Hurl himself straight upon the awful goal.
Oh ! then as if to spare the o'erstrained sight,
A wonder happened for that gazing host ;
For scarcely had the impious Vivero
Chosen his course, and fixed his forceful aim.—
When lo ! he vanished like the thinnest flake
Of tenuous snow upon a sea of fire.

   Long days they watched in vain for any sign ;
They knew not whether he did reach and pierce
The glowing cover of that orbic shrine,
Or had been quenched forever from the world.

   One morn, when Music's circuit was again
Complete, and truant Peace once more restrained
Within the magic line, they saw on high,
Above their rescued world, a small, dark cloud,
A thing not seen before in solar skies ;

And as it floated o'er their radiant heads,
There shone upon it seven blended rings
Of sacred colors, of such wondrous size,
They knew they were the same that Vivero
Had worn upon his arm.   They watched the cloud
Fall slowly down into the nether deeps,
Bearing that pure, immortal emblem still
Upon its folds, until it sank entombed
Into that darkened world we called the moon,
When we surveyed it from the earth : and still
That fadeless circlet may be often seen
Coiled round that starry grave in largest woe
Or, shredless, groping in the wastes of storms.
TINTA.   O 'tis a wondrous tale !   What other orb
Hath such a history that its excess,
Which liveth only in remembered speech,
Holds stories such as this?   Poor Vivero !
Were it no wrong to our beloved Lord,
How I could pity thee !   But gods are stern
To guilt of arrogance : and they forgive
Their erring people any fault but this.

    Tell me, dear teacher, shall we ever see
That being we adore?—I mean not here,
Nor soon, but shall we *ever* see our Lord ?
In some far time, and from some distant sphere,
If that inviolate veil were drawn away,
Should we dare look, with furtive, timid eyes,
Downward upon him?

ARDO.   Nay, a nearer place
Crave I for thee and me !   Be reverent,
But fear thou not, nor overstretch thine awe ;
For I believe that our great Sovereign's shield
Doth slowly waste between the crossing heat
Of his own central and our outward zeal ;
That it doth furnish stuff for our good deeds,
And when all good is done, will fade away
And leave revealed the perfect one within,
Who henceforth shall remain as one of us.

  But now, refreshed, we must once more to work ;—
Put on thy sandals of embalmèd flame :
Bind up again the loosened amber filaments
Of thine abundant hair, lest thou appear
Too glorious amongst thine elder sisters :
Let go the hidden rudder of thine eyes,
Which makes them ever keep their course towards me ;
And I will pluck Love's pharos from mine own,
Which thou art sailing by.   And now those eyes
Too long reduced to visions of one soul,
Again must gauge themselves to multitudes ;
And from the verges of dispersion's deeps,
Strain after gods.   Now take my hand and come ;
We will away to my most precious spring,
And thou shalt drink one draught from mine own hand,
And there together will we, singing, mix
Such potent liquor for the earth's dry cup,
That none shall be there more athirst for joy,
And all be thence informed of our sweet love.

THE COMMON MAN.

Behold ! he daily does the world's wide will,
Makes what is good, and masters what is ill :
Lives not oblivious of earth's blessed ways,
Nor clogs his progress with disordered days.

His strength is as the braces of the sky,
And as the salt sea's breath his bravery ;
His own worth knows he and its true intents,
Although he counts not its constituents.

His arms are round and full with deeds unwrought,
His shoulders mighty and abased by nought :
For they can bear, nor press upon the heart,
What cowards cast there with eluding art.

Justice and mercy do in him concur :
His truth is as the day's diameter ;
And Peace between his eyes doth have her seat,
Like to a queen between two handmaids sweet.

What man has ever done he doeth now—
Be it to forge, to build, to sow or plow—
And round the forefront of his last act shine
The cumulate beauties of the long design.

Not in the new alone doth beauty sleep,
For olden things a higher import keep ;
That stream is purest which doth longest flow,
And what is best will aye the farthest go.

The common man is slow, sees not afar ;
Must keep his eyes where'er his full hands are :
Enjoys the common hues of near-by things ;
Stops at the blue of mystic quiverings.

His goals are near, and one the sun each day
Drops warm with life and not too far away ;
But ere the night he grasps the bauble sweet,
And its sun-warmth is blent with his heart's heat.

Yet not the slave of despot day is he,
But the free servant of the Century ;
And though she wears her veil upon her face,
He sometimes feels her hand's imperial grace.

He sees the measure of his lasting might
In every work his hand concludes aright ;
And each result his widening spirit frees ;—
The houses he has built hold but his families.

His lips have simple songs, while Music's art
Doth only still the groves about his heart ;
That when her chosen chantress sings, at last,
No rival songs shall 'gainst that strain be cast.

Not from rare moments' tenuous chalices,
Flame-filled and flashing with infinities,
But from a common cup of cumbrous clay
Drinks he the lasting joys of his long day.

No fairies light upon his steps attend,
But giant, heavy-handed forms, that bend
And pour for him thick liquids, amber-clear,
Slow drip of sweets long stored from some dream year.

Yet there is set within his heavy frame
A secret truth which hath on earth no name :
And though his lips shall speak wise things and true,
His words have one side dark and give no clew.

He is the keeper of all permanencies ;
On his acceptance wait discoveries ;—
Though one should force a gift from Heaven's height,
The common man alone can keep it bright.

He has long leisure, yet he wastes no time :
He waxes old, but still enjoys his prime :
And what another in despair has sought,
He finds, at last, without one troublous thought.

Behold ! he daily does the world's wide will :
Makes what is good, and masters what is ill :
And when the race has reached its earthly span,
The *common* shall appear the *perfect* man.

THE MUSIC OF GRAVES.

There never was heart of a man,
    But a song in it longed to be sung ;
Nor ever a brain that began,
    But a glimmer of truth was there flung.
O woe, to the lips that were mute !
    O woe, for the false words said !
For with naught but the grave for a lute
    True song must now come from the dead.

O come to this new-made grave,
    And quicken its great, dull strings ;
That the rigid lips which the death-peace crave
    May loosen the music that clings.
O call to the wind and the rain !
    O call to the heat or the frost !
To gather the whispers of pain,
    Lest the song of the dead should be lost.

THE CHRISTMAS TABLE.

Now bring the ample table out,
  And have the cloth well laid ;
And load the board, if so thou canst,
  With what thyself hast made ;
    That every guest
    Shall find the best
For which his heart has prayed.

Then set thou, at the table's head,
  A chair of sable state ;
And let each one, with reverence say :
  "Come Christ, here is no hate :"
    And the Denied,
    The Crucified,
Shall leave His cross, though late.

But set thou, at the table's foot,
  A chair of equal grace ;
That the new Christ of perfect life
  May see, with shining face :
    See, from some height,
    Its spotless white,
And come and take his place.

THE TWO DISCOVERIES.

I

"Twas with such eyes
  As every mortal hath,
When clear surprise
  Lightens the path,
That she beheld
  His spirit rise :—
That she did see
  Its august size
Matching nobility.
  "Twas only as
The others saw
  The man he was,
That she, with awe,
  Beheld Love pass.

II

"Twas with the sight
  The few possess
Who see the right,
  Who know to bless ;
That she beheld,

After the glory waned,
The glory still :——
   That there remained,
After the thrill,
   The conscious heart
To know and claim,
   From his great deed apart,
The *man* in shame.
'Twas not what others see
   That now she saw,——
Splendor and majesty,
   Things without flaw :
But, with a finer sight
   Than takes the swift delight,
When in full view,
   Grand Love goes by :
She subtly knew
   Plain Love who waited nigh.

THE VALKYRIES.

Directors of the launchèd death !
Receivers of the latest breath !
How did ye choose the guests for Odin's hall ?
On whom were your first favors wont to fall ?
    Who'er it be that answereth,
Say why ye chose a king and why his thrall.

Loved ye the most who slew the most ?
Was that fierce one your chosen ghost,
Whose battle axe always the deepest went ;—
Whose bloody spear was aye the farthest sent ?
    Who, being dead, still made his boast,
And cheered the weary flight with fury yet unspent ?

Had ye no thought for him whose blade
Shone like a thing that hath no shade,
And firmer temper took at every blow,
From subtle currents which therewith did flow ;
    And not alone the hand obeyed,
But struck most righteously, the guilty foe ?

And spared ye any in that time
Of brutal deed, of blood and grime,

For that they were beloved by ladies fair,
And sent sweet songs across the trumpet's blare?
       Nay! seemed it not a crime,
To hinder those whose loves were all their care?

       How choose ye *now* your sacred dead?—
       Where once was war is peace instead.
Have your own hearts not gathered newer clews,
Seeing how earthly maids the living choose?
       Are not your white lips turned more red?
Have not your eyes been purged with sweeter views?

       Yea! hath not Odin, your great Sire,
       Been tutored to a new desire?
Hath not some signal from a human hand
Startled the warders of that ghostly land,
       That now a new and softer fire
They burn, with reverence, all along the strand?

THE DEAD DAY.

I made a tryst with a coming day ;
    A day yet far away ;
        And I said :
"I will meet thee, O day, on the hills !
    When thy glory the east overfills.
    Let thy sisters before thee regret !
        And thy sisters behind thee despair !
For I'll bring thee a joy which the world cannot fret :
I will show thee the worth which the heavens declare ;
        A *perfect heart* will I bear."

    But the red of her coming turned gray :
        For I was far away :
            And she said :
    "Let me die with the longing that kills ;
        Which through the dead heart ever thrills !"
    Then upon the low bier was she set,
        And borne through the shivering air,
By her maidens all darksome and wet ;
While wails of defeat were still echoing there,
        And a broken heart was in prayer.

THE LAGGARD.

So swift passed by him the people, so seldom looked
    they around,
They saw not the face of the laggard, whose feet on the
    covetous ground
Found rest and a lingering lightness and delight as of
    lasting good,
And slower and slower proceeded until it seemed that
    he stood.
But hurried the many onward in broken masses and
    groups,
And the hollows and empty spaces of their frenzy's
    serpent-loops
Seemed spectral hearts of excitement with their fever
    and force pulsed out :
Their birth the death of a moment, their death the birth
    of a shout.
At ease the loiterer followed, untouched by the strug-
    gling throng,
For multitudes feel a repulsion from souls that are
    silent and strong ;
And nothing is half so defended as the simple peace of
    the heart,

Since tumult can never adventure save where it already
    is part.
He moved in the lull of their strivings, in the realms
    of relapse and spent breath,
Where the forces wasted of mortals return again unto
    death ;
And his progress was that of a planet with a new
    immortal light,
Which sails with a steadfast glory through the wrecks
    of a stellar night.
Attrition ravaged their faces and only as shifting sands
Were the changes ever upon them—Confusion alone
    commands ;
But *his* had the glow of creation, and its motions all
    were combined
To picture the single endeavor of the sovereign, single
    mind ;
And every angel of beauty some gift on that face did lay,
For up from his heart no demon ever rose to drive
    it away.
Their hope was a self-shivered mirror, each piece
    showed a different face ;
While his was a casket made ready for the gem that
    awaited its place.
The bows of their hearts, like to galleys, were beaked
    for the struggles of hate,
And sundered and sank each pleasure before they had
    taken its freight ;

His heart was a delicate life-boat with a roseate sail
　　unfurled,
And saving one joy undiminished it sailed the whole
　　of the world.
Their desire was a passionate craving to feel all the
　　forces that are,
So long as was left on their spirits one spot for sensation
　　to scar ;
While to fathom the single impression and its subtle
　　folds unwind,
Was enough for his truer longing, enough for his single
　　mind ;
For he knew that his spacious being, unloosed to its
　　farthest curve,
Lacked room for that one revelation, though he held it
　　all in reserve.
The future to them was a straight thread spun from the
　　mists of the past,
Which, miserly, marked out before them the way which
　　they traveled so fast ;
And the present had no existence, or seemed, past any
　　dispute,
But the little line that lapses 'tween the raised and
　　lowered foot ;
While time to the leal-hearted laggard had no dispersion
　　of soul,
Could only, starlike, around him its widening circles
　　roll ;

And the growing plane of its orbit was the present unto
him,
Where life in a lustrous glory stretched calmly away
to its rim.

But the running line of their hasting, like the chain in
the deep, cool well,
At last drew speech from the silence wherein such
spirits dwell ;
And turning about to the nearest he showed them the
peace of his face,
And by the power of his purpose checked the speed of
their fevered pace.
Then suddenly ended their ravings, with the shock of a
sharp surprise,
As a storm might halt in its fury with quick reverence
in its eyes,
If right in its path there shimmered, with no watchmen
stationed around,
A colony of glorious angels just arrived to inhabit the
ground.
And these are the words he uttered unto such as lingered
anear,
Amazed and afraid and attracted and half unwilling
to hear.
"Why haste ye on Change's worn pinions to the eyry
of lusting and madness?
Why float in the storm-winds of laughter to the dreary
expanses of sadness?

Do ye have the deep heavens for your hasting, as the
    birds in their joyous projection?
Are the white doves of Heaven abandoned, with their
    burdens of mystic reflection,
To the clutch of the hawk or the falcon or some other
    felonious capture,
While the heart that is looking and longing shall miss of
    its infinite rapture?
Can the racers of commonest craving run as fast as the
    coursers etherial
Which the heart sends afar in its calmness, and guideth
    with reins immaterial?
Ye but follow false birds of illusion from the nests of
    your own living treasures ;
And ye gather from falsehood's beguilement that which
    falsehood's memory measures.
Ye are following vanishing pictures and dancing shadows
    and splendors
By a mock sun scornfully scattered, when the spirit,
    unwitting, surrenders
Both the earth and the sky of its being, where the forces
    creative are hidden ;
And the thing ye might form into beauty, unto hideous
    shapes shall be bidden.
Like as golden wheels ye are whirling o'er highways
    poluted by passion,
And the mud-drops ever thrown forward seem to you of
    an exquisite fashion :—

Were they drops from the car of old Neptune ere the
    waters of ocean were bitter,
Or a shower from a cloudlet begotten where the mists
    with divinity glitter,
Ye could not more eager pursue them or struggle the
    harder to catch them ;
And the things that with them are mingled to illumine
    and visibly match them,
Are the floating sparkles and relics of your thought's
    first pure creations,
Comminuted and mangled in folly and left for the
    laughter of nations.
But what is the gain of your hasting?—all your craving
    and envious malice?
Doth not violence spill without scruple the sweets of the
    spiritual chalice?
Yet ally yourselves with the whirlwind, let riot fecundate
    the spirit,
And the thing that is brought forth in frenzy, though ye
    shuddering strive not to rear it,
Shall for ages ravage your beings, uprooting and smiting
    and rending,
Until there is left a mere desert, and death or dark
    horror impending.
But if what ye are seeking is precious, and it seemeth
    dearer and dearer,
Will the smoked glass succor your vision? or your
    breath on the pane make it clearer?

Have ye fear that some others should gather your
    delights ere your hearts have possessed them?
Then, in truth, were they yours by their nature, from
    the demons themselves ye could wrest them!
Oh! unseemly these struggles and racings, when to love
    is the whole that is needed;
Since the heart knows to carry you farther than the feet
    of man e'er proceeded.
Doth befit your false fury a being, who hath through the
    empyrean whitened,
And o'erflown the sun in his splendor nor endured that
    his garments were brightened?
Who hath dared to the hazardous borders of the regions
    starless and rangeless,
Where the breezes so friendly to flying lie as dead at the
    feet of the Changeless?
Fear ye now to repose in the ether which is still in your
    spirits' recesses,
And if lulled to the stillness of Heaven, with the passage
    of angels still blesses?
Do ye fear, unless always it's flashing, that the heart's
    fiery lightnings shall wither,
And when summoned to shatter some darkness be too
    feeble to carry you thither?
But, behold! how the passionate patience of the flower
    by the roadside there growing,
In the colorless air finds and fixes the shy sweets that
    forever are flowing:

Let us sit down there in the coolness and surround it in
    reverent wonder ;
We can love that flower together and might fail to so
    love what is yonder :
We shall hear if we peacefully listen, as they cordially
    signal each other,
'Cross the dreary spaces of clamor, in such tones as
    nothing can smother,
The bright band of immaculate lovers, with a sweet and
    solemn insistence,
Moulding ever to trumpeting actions the clear metal of
    perfect existence.
And at night shall we tent us securely in the strength
    which belongs to endurance,
And the light of the undying spirit shall burn for the
    pilgrim's assurance ;
And shall frighten the forces of darkness, while against
    all the tempest's assailing,
From the heart's still recesses shall issue counter-blasts
    of command never failing ;
And soon shall the lover-guest find us,—shall approach
    and the sleepers awaken ;
And the fear in the heart still abiding, from its loosened
    beats shall be shaken.

THE TWO CLAIMANTS.

Two spirits late were poised above this land,
Mother of Nations, Spirit of the World :
And like a mist across the heavens' sheen
Spread the effect of counter-working wills.
For not agreement's sweet convergences
To some effulgent embouchure in air,
Had brought these mighty beings face to face ;
But discord's hidden snare at crossing ways.
A skyey winter grew about the spot,
And the chilled light fell through the boreal air,
In ghostly flakes which drifted round their feet.

And she, the Mother of Nations called, did hold
A chart of States before her, and across
The folding glory of her vivid dress—
Less ample than the other's though it seemed—
Flickered dark lines that made a ghastly web,
And seemed reflections of the shifting boundaries
Which circumscribed her daughters' earthly realms.
Her eyes also seemed weary with the chase
Of those elusive lines which were as seams
Upon the mended vestments of the earth,
And when she spoke, the crystal waves of speech

Seemed broken into many tinted arcs
And sweet deceitful rings, to fit the ear
Reserved for charm of tender confidence ;
But in her full and uncurbed majesty,
Stood her companion there, and her clear voice
Enfolded worlds within its fluent curves,
E'en as an Iris-bow bent to a circle.

    And, listening, I heard the lesser Power
First urge her thought and thus proclaim her right :
"Mine and my children's still remains the earth !
I was here *first* of all who dwell in space,
When out from the invisible there rolled
This emerald wonder !   Is't as nought,
That I first felt this whirling glory draw
My heart to unknown motions and to new desires?—
That its sweet airs did blow their first delights
Across my face? or that my daring feet
First touched the bending tips of its green turf?
Yea ! gained I then no new prerogative—
No lasting grace that will prevail on high—
That gliding through its groves and following
The coaxing current of a tuneful stream,
I first beheld, with unapprenticed eyes,
That riddle of the world—that sweet surprise
Of gods—a *man* ; did meet him face to face,
And looked into his eyes—his human eyes—
And heard his first uncertain words of love
Unto a woman, greater mystery?"

Then answered her the strong World Spirit thus :
"Thy boasted right hath never been denied ;
And, yet, methinks, thou hast asserted it,
As though that perfect-sailing orb had been
A sinking wreck, and some swift aid of thine
Had gained a ceaseless right of salvage to it.
Yet hath thy doubtful claim been e'er allowed,—
Opposed by none, though acquiesence made
A grief too large for Sorrow's greatest gauge.
What hast thou done with this vast privilege ?
What, save to weave thy web of boundaries
Around a world designed for liberty ?
Thou couldst not even *see* thy spheric prey,
Except as it did, curve by curve, revolve
Across thy narrow sight : thou couldst but be
A slow explorer there, and, one by one,
Inscribe the parts upon thy needful chart ;
Or catch their outlines on thy sullied robes
More spacious than thy narrow vision was.
And thou didst quickly drive lorn waifs of space
Down through the earth's clear air and through dim
        ways
Of earthly generation to become
Thy misbegotten offspring, and the bane
Of man enmeshed for them ! What right hadst thou
To cut the bond of human unity,
And put the separate ends within their hands,
To tangle them with enmity ?   But know

Now, for I say it, that thou hast done ill !
Thou hast outlived thy right ! To me doth fall
Thy forfeited estate ! Go now, dismiss
Thy children from their places to again
Roam restless through blank space as yet unstrewn
With worlds."

Now for a long space did I hear no word,
And then the other spoke the untried speech
Of pain. "O States and Empires of the earth,
Ye are my children ! slow-transformed,
In the vast womb of Cycles, into shapes
Which bear my image :—ye are very fruits
Of my maternity ! What mother else,
Hath reared in such alarms her progeny ?
How in your separate and remote abodes
Have I protected, e'er unfailingly,
All you my nurslings ! how, from the first hour,
Have I endeavoured to tear wholly off
All taint of former vagrancy in space,
And train you to the regions definite
Of solid and enduring happiness !
How have I run to shield you at all times !
When spiteful demons have made war on you,
What side have I left without saving guard ?
Though they have mined the quiet earth and dropped
Germs of convulsions there, to rend apart
Your rocky fastnesses : though they have bent

The mountains to a bow, to launch at you
Their frozen thunders, or have stamped
The soft air hard, to hurl wide furies down
Upon your heads ; yea, though most impiously
They have unloosed those seizures dire of strange
And dreadful maladies, which spread 'mongst men
Destructive frenzies :—yet it was my joy
To ever be with you.   But all my flights
Around your cherished realms, have left no loops
Of living concord which a hostile word
Of tyrant-spirit breaks not !   Nought remains,
But that far fellowship of space, which seems,
To those who have but played at human love,
Only as solitude.   I cannot hold you !

O India who droopest so the head,
And thickenest the air into a dusk,
With the dark fragrance of thy favored flower,
For mid-day dreams ; wake not for my farewell !
O would that I might join thee in that sleep
Which feeds alone upon sweet memories,
And will not pass at touch of present grief,
Though grief should turn itself to burning suns.
        And thou Italia, who sitt'st at ease
Upon the sun-ward side of thy vast ruins,
And idly watchest swarms of little folk
At play before thee : hop'st thou still, O child,
For future heroes to delight those eyes

Which only shine for demigods? Nay, turn
Thy face around and chase the mighty shades
Who fly from thee ! Haste now, and fare thee well !
Farewell to thee Britania, ever young !
Thou who hast made a never-ending pact
With dawn and sunset, equi-distant powers,
To keep their heart-hues on thy face at noon ;
Who hast put portions of thy realm far off,
To show how easily thy regnant will
Can leap the vast and hostile intervals,
Or to enjoy perpetual interchange
Of sweet salutes with the remote—the dark—
And train the heart to tender prophecies ;—
Oh, boundless woe ! that thou must now forsake
These eyes and go where neither sound of voice
Nor divination may take hold of thee.
    And now to thee Columbia, I speak,
Sublime and dreadful offspring of mine age !
Thou wild, unfilial child ! Keepest thou still
That face turned from me ? Hidest it for shame
That sorrow hath no faint impression there,
Or art thou e'en unconscious of my voice ?
I feel a mystery of reverence
Creep, like a vapor, o'er the lucid streams
Of the affections, darkening their course ;
But vague and doubting guesses of thy thought
Haunt the vast spaces of my unfilled life,
And bid me still to love thee, though in fear.

Now let Farewell drop her dark curtain down
Between thy secret and my auguries ;
Yet would I, that, in some far, secret time,
Welcome might ring that curtain up again,
And show thee true protagonist of earth.
　　　Now all my children whom I have not named,
Farewell ! farewell ! Fade, sink away ! henceforth
Ye are but ghosts :—wan spectres which will haunt
All drear domains of space, and on the air
Of that new world I soon shall go to seek,
Work dim alarms and subtle shiverings."

　　Soon as the grieving spirit ceased her plaint,
The Spirit of the World, with pity moved,
Spoke thus : "O erring sister, be consoled !
Let such a change go o'er thy sudden globe
Of woe, as thou shalt see pass pleasantly
Around the circles of the quickened earth,
When I shall speak to it. Soon shalt thou see
How shrunken man hath sore offended us,
Who had the power to see his destiny.
And thou shalt find new joy, when he doth turn
His *perfect* face unto thee ; thou shalt know
The beauty of a human face, when all
The glory which has settled round the heart
Shall rise like white flame through the eased life,
And pour immortal graces in the fount
Of smiles ; when all the sun-glow drenching earth,

And all the crimson fervors of its heart,
Combine in fertile juices which shall feed
No growing thing, except the flower of song,
Which reaches ever to man's sacred lips.
There is but *one* humanity ; and man—
Yea ! every man—must have the whole of earth,
To be himself as whole.   Thou hast done ill,
To so divide men into hostile groups,
That each must keep his eyes fixed on the *few*,
And no one is allowed to turn his face
Toward the slow-shaping wonder, true Mankind,
And force that darksome giant to disclose
The perfect image worn upon his heart.
Thou hast restrained their sight to vortices,
Whose outer rim is boundary of their state,
And all whose lessening circles end, at last,
In the sunk centre-point of selfish appetite.
But *I* will train men's vision to the curves
Of earth, and, like a sea-fowl o'er the waves,
Shall it, with dip and rise, fly 'cross the land ;
And I will teach them to restore the earth
To its first beauty, and to add their own
Unto it ; yet will tell them that all space
Is theirs ; and that they must so fling themselves
Into that larger realm, and so transfuse
It with their buoyant blessedness, that soon,
Their little earth shall seem a flowery ball
Which trooping spirits carry in their hands.

THE LAST PRAYER.

To the bare summit of a wooded hill,
Close to the church whose altars he had served
The years since manhood had dethroned the gods
Of pagan infancy, went heavily
An old priest, sorrowful of heart and sore
With frequent recoil of unanswered prayer.
There, for a long time, stood he silently,
With eyes that turned them many times around
The circling scope of sky, as if they wound
Some light coil of the heart's expectancy
Round the included world to prison it,
Or hold it for his leisure's after-search.
At length, with tearful face upraised, he spoke.

"God, I have waited with still lips, for fear
Mine own words might irreverently invade
The chambers of mine ear, and claim the space
Thine own would share with none, unless divine.
Now speak, I pray Thee, lest mine ear do feed
So long on silence that no sound again
Have power to waken it !

                          How many years
Have but the wasted echoes of Thy voice

Sufficed me ! For how many voiceless years,
Have nought but misty cloudlets of the far
And thunderous waterfall of speech divine,
Floated the dumb void through of dreariness !
How has my thin hair whitened o'er the black
Despair of the heart, because Thou heardst me not !
I do beseech Thee now for but one word !
That I may know, full surely, whether it
Were formed above a heart or no.   If *now*
Thou dost not speak, I fear Thou never wilt
When I am shamed amidst the deities
Who spread Thy presence in some other world.
But tell me, God, where I may hear Thy voice !
Is it where bright and busy lightnings whet
The earth's sharp peaks to keen attentiveness ?
Or where the mountains hold themselves apart
To make Thee all sufficing room to lay
The broad front of Thy words in ? Is it where
The world has given up some feet of earth
To Thee, and wrought opinion into stone
To cover it, and set men up to watch
For Thee, with thrifty lie-inwoven lips
Well-bated with old words of Thine, to catch
Thy newer voice with ? Nay ! that, in sooth,
Is but the hunter's clumsy art, and Thou
Wilt suffer no pursuit.   Have I not stood
There while the shadow-dropping years,
Like woods, were beaten for their quarry, till

Mine ears grew weary with the lengthened chase,
And Echo was aggrieved for want of new,
Sweet words? But I have pitied her, and brought
The strong restoratives of lusty shout
And robust laugh and song such as the street
Doth often feed her with.

          And I have prayed
To Echo before now, what time mine ear
Was strained with striving for Thy distant voice,
Thinking that she might take some subtle sound
Of message which mine ears took not, and would
Repeat it louder unto me.

          O God,
I *know* Thou *art*,' although Thou shunnest me,
And speakest not, nor show'st Thy face ; but yet
I thank Thee I am no philosopher !
I do not care to make a name to stamp
My ignorance on ; I would not undertake
To placard mysteries and think them better known.
To build a wall around the night, would not
Make any star more bright ; and why then build ?
I cannot stop to *make* Thee ere I speak,
Or make excuse for Thee as one who lacks
Some godlike quality men may discern ;
I would not view the shadow of myself,
Thrown forward on the bank of mingled glooms

That is the future, and pay homage to it ;
I would not so misprize Thee as to call
Prevision of the perfect self, true God ;
Nor would I so disperse Thee through the world
That Thou art robbed of that sweet attribute,
Dearest to man, the personal life of self ;
I only feel Thee *God*, and see Thy power
Working superiorly beside mine own.

There may be higher Gods than Thou ; let be !
That makes the need of Thee no less for earth
Where Thou art dominant.   Yet know I not
What rights and offices exclusively
Are Thine in this commingling life ; I fail
To disentangle, fairly, Thine from mine,
When, in his every task, Thou deign'st to be
Co-laborer with man ; I cannot find,
Within me, or without, or anywhere,
The simple, pure, etherial element
Of God, dissociate, and Himself alone.
I cannot see Thee ; but Thy presence here
Moves on some subtler sense than sight, with touch,
Broader than mine own being—larger far
Than nature which surrounds and only seems
But as Thy finger on me : till the soul
Thrilling with all the beauties of the world
Assures itself of Thee exultantly.

Yea, God, I know that Thou art beautiful !
The faded images of Thee which men
Have drawn upon the surface of the rough
Conglomerate of their mingled hopes and fears,—
How can I own them? how can I revere
The phantom shapes of sickly ecstasies,
Wherein some human worth doth often die,
To leave a ghost to figure as a God?
How less than hate those color-clad conceits
Which stare at me so boldly from the walls,
When I rehearse Thy sacred mysteries,
And touch the symbols of Thee, in the hush
Between loud heart-beats? Even in the free
And boundless treasury of sweet things
Where now I stand, I dare not contemplate
These earthly charms and sky dependencies,
As types of Thee or any part of Thee :
Thinking, mayhap, the flowers, fields and birds
And cloud accompaniment of the days
Progressive pagentry, might closer be
Unto the beauty of this human heart,
Than unto Thee—for I do here maintain
That man has his own beauty e'en as God—
But my best witness to Thy beauty, stands
The soul interpreting each beauteous thing
As but a guide to Thee, although Thou yet
Dost hide Thyself before me as I seek.
    But dost Thou so love silence that no word

May be vouchsafed to me, who wait so long?
Live there then other Gods to talk with Thee,
And canst Thou not forsake, for but this once,
The long entrancement of their speech to say
One word to me, who hearest but earthly words?
Is't then that the large import of Thy words
Out-reaches the divided day of man,
And that to hear Thy briefest utterance,
Must one live on uninterruptedly,
In a broad plane of open consciousness,
While night and sleep, forced back by might of self,
Mount slowly in black drifts on either hand?
Or is Thy voice dispersed in separate tones,
Throughout the whole of nature, so that each
That uttereth sound in all the living world,
Doth speak the word of God?   O then recall
The scattered and disordered filaments
Of fluent speech, and reunited, pour
The whole supernal flood upon my soul,
Though there be silence in both earth and Heaven,
And speech comes never more from these old lips !

It is believed that Thou aforetime spoke
To chosen men, who heard Thee reverently ;—
Deliver now one word to me, that I
May show Thee how those patriarchal saints
Did shorten hearing to a vulgar mark
And offered Thee contempt of common ear ;

For I will listen to Thee as a god,
Although my speech is spotted o'er with earth !
Shall I believe the sacred histories,
Which say that Thou didst really speak to *them*,
If Thou refusest now to speak to *me*?
Had olden men the watchword to God's house,
And I and other men of this new time,
Not gain admission for communion there?
Was then Thy speech a favor of Thy grace,
Or quick concession to discovery
Of secret, subterranean ways to Thee?
Lingers there yet, with latent potency,
Amidst the debris of disrupted speech,
Some magic reliquary of old words
Which once were fitly used to summon God with?
What lack I then of that sufficiency
Which pleasedst Thee in them?   Is it *against*
Or *for* us of to-day, that what was thought
Thy very word, hath mingled with the world
These many thousand years? that I have heard
It three score years and more, and reverently
Have worn my lips with it, dost Thou adjudge
Me now less worthy of an audience?
"Twere better, Thou hadst *never* spoken then !
Dost Thou attribute it as guilt to me,
That when my lips have uttered forth the words
Alleged of Thee, I did not visibly
Put on the aspect of divinity—

The awful splendors of a god that grew
More godlike in the work of putting truth
Of Heaven in earthly words—to then and there,
Perform the miracle of making speech
Of man transpierce man's shield of habitudes,
And reach the soul, as reached it that first word
That through the clearness of the virgin air
Did fall upon it? Nay, I could not help
That men should see the common man that stood
Behind Thy words, and give a careless ear
Unto Thy minister! I could not help
That men should come as if to see Thy face,
And only see some unetherial light
Upon the far side of their sins, and shamed
Thee, being satisfied that it was God!
Yet be not wroth with me, Thy servitor,
For their insensibility; or that
They left the dust upon me of dead hearts!

Still silent, God! or dost Thou speak in vain?
Is then my soul so bounden to mine ear,
That its choked channels stop Thine ample voice?
Nay, now I am as one disbodied quite!
I have no past! I am become a child,
With flight of eagle added! from the white
Self-lighted burning of my rising heart,
Experience, like a smoke, doth roll away,
And every fond remembrance of old joys

Doth die to send an incense unto Thee !
I make clear space around my naked soul,
That Thou mayst drop one word into the void !"

Here ended his wild prayer ; and following,
Was no sound manifest of any kind,
Save only his own sobbing ; as if awe
Of that assuageless grief held all things mute.
At last the old man turned his white face down
Towards the great church he had ascended from,
But recognized it not for foreignness ;
Then down the hill's remoter side did pass.

THE WONDERFUL WORKMEN.

Four men met in an open field,
  When awe still held the stars away,
Although the sun had, sated, reeled
  Down from the ivory peaks of day.

Workmen they were, but work had left
  Them all unwearied as at dawn ;
For strength is always safe from theft,
  Unless weak sloth is guardian.

A farmer, mason, weaver made
  The first three of this company ;
The fourth pursued as good a trade,—
  The high one of ship-carpentry.

Noble and grave these four men seemed ;
  Dauntless, calm-voiced and vision-taught ;
The light which from their pure eyes streamed
  Had long run by the shores of thought.

Their eyes were serious, earnest eyes,
  Like those which reverent Wonder leads ;
As though they long, with spirits wise,
  Had walked behind the noblest deeds.

Their spirits' toils did never stop,
  And when their rude tools they laid by,
They seized the ones the angels drop
  When they draw near the Deity.

Eternal power flowed away
  From their great hearts on every side :
The labor of their hands by day,
  Was but the drift upon that tide.

The life they knew was unconfined,
  And so surpassed the frame that delves,
That they appeared to human-kind
  As cordial comrades of themselves.

No weight of self was on their hands,
  And light as life their potent touch ;
For Nature hears the heart's commands,
  And all things earthly yield to such.

And all the varied implements,
  Which felt each day their noble grasp,
Answered the firm hands pure intents,
  And knew at once the double clasp.

These workmen never toiled for bread,
  Though living bread they never lacked ;—
It grew where'er their labor led,
  And sent a stalk from every act.

They worked for joy, for well they knew
  That joy but marked their spirits' sway ;
And if they took the wages due,
  They took that they might throw away.

They worked because their hearts were strong,
  And others seemed more weak than they ;
They worked to lessen every wrong
  On kindred hearts that heavy lay.

They worked to break the bands of need,
  That drew the fairest souls awry ;
They worked to substitute, with speed,
  The leisure of love's sunbeam tie.

They worked to fashion silent roads
  From out their pent hearts' deadening din ;
That from their far-off, blest abodes,
  The peaceful spirits might come in.

How great the joy, as these men meet,
  Flows full into their beings' core !
Each as his neighbor he doth greet,
  Feels all the perfect joy of four.

They know each other at first sight,
  And their embrace endureth long ;
They hear each other with delight,
  And each doth tell his tale in song.

SONG OF THE SHIP-CARPENTER.

Here me well ! dear brothers three ;
My craft is good and my heart is free ;
  I build ships of firmest plank,
And many have stroked the sinking sea,
  But never yet one sank.

Many voyages have I gone
Upon each ship before 'twas done ;
  Many a time have spread the sails,
And travelled swifter than the sun,
  Afar till ocean fails.

There was no crew upon the deck ;
I only, manned my seeming wreck
  Unbuilded yet to perfect form ;
No rock beneath the wave could check,
  Nor ever any storm.

Thus afloat each vessel grew,
Sea and storm tried each piece new ;
  And their protection first was given,
And love was sworn and pledges true,
  Before a bolt was driven.

The winds and waves accept my float ;
Their nature breathe in every boat,—
  Breathe speed and scorn of docks ;

And many gentle guides devote,
  For risk of rocks.

Upon the apex of the sea,
Where all the waves do well agree
  To not abandon any shore,
But flow each way impartially ;
  There often do I moor.

And all the waves I tie together,—
Tie with a loose and loving tether ;
  Which yet shall hold like bands of steel,
In summer or in winter weather,
  'Neath my ship's keel.

Then speak I to the willing waves,
And tell them what my sad heart craves ;
  And bid them say to every beach,
A ship shall come that nothing saves,
  But hath a gift for each.

And bid them cry to all souls there,
To hasten with continuous care,
  To find the freight that ne'er was told
By hand that hurts or makes despair,
  Into a vessel's hold ;—

The freight which once a ship of state,
First bore away from Heaven's gate—

Life's love-encircling zone—
But lost upon some shore of hate,
    The place unknown.

THE SONG OF THE WEAVER.

My work is weaving, and my kin
    Are those who weave and those who spin ;
But most of all my kindred are
    The loomless weavers near and far.
Whose fabrics pure and bright and thin,
    Would clothe a hope or robe a star.

There's one who weaves the rain-bow wreath,
    Which dying furies do bequeath
To the departing storm-cloud's heir ;
    And one who weaves the flushes rare,
Which flicker o'er flame's lambent sheath,
    And 'cross the restless lightning's lair.

Beneath the moon's low canopy.
    Some slumberous weavers lie ;
In dreams they weave the raiment bright,
    By fairy worn and favored sprite,
As down to earth they radiant fly,
    To consecrate the fane of night.

Another, the dawn weaver, weaves
    The sacrificial dress the earth receives,
When comes in person the adored one

To tend his altar of the sun ;
And penitence again achieves
Day fresh as the fount of Helicon.

And one there is, who, near the skies,
Weaves glamours for all lovers' eyes,
And weaves, oh, wondrous art ! besides,
White visions of the sanctified ;
Which swifter than the eagles rise,
And widen as the heavens are wide.

Each is my comrade, each my teacher ;
The sun also, the downward-reacher ;
Who blends in Nature's ceaseless loom,
The earth's sad shade with his own bloom ;
And helpeth most the pale beseecher,
Who kneeleth in her western room.

And though I may not weave as they,
Yet work I in my cloth each day,
Some cunning threads which ne'er were spun
By flower-wheel from the heart of the sun ;
And many subtle plans I lay,
That all my cloth be fairly done.

I would that all who shall it wear,
Might find that it will never tear ;
That every heart which beats below
The fabric I have woven so,

Shall touch the spring and feel the snare.
    And swiftly all the others know.

From Morning's face or Evening's mask,
    I take new virtue for my task :
And better threads I often gain
    Where saints have wept or angels lain :
And every gentle thing I ask
    For floss from its soft skein.

Although I can, with all my care,
    Weave not what pure immortals wear,
I yet may form the fabric meet
    To lie beneath their hovering feet ;
And that shall keep me from despair,
    Until I die, if death be fleet.

SONG OF THE FARMER.

In the house of the foliate forces,
    I am only a favorite servant :
But my service is free as the water-courses,
    And my love for my lords is fervent.
See these arms and these hands that in seasons unnum-
        bered
    My masters with treasures have cumbered ;
Strong to swing lightly their ponderous doors,
    Strong to sweep often their measureless floors ;
And with ease I can manage the broad furrow-shutter,
    Through which their fringe-flowing draperies flutter.

How arose this body so mighty and massive?
  Have some deities wrought while I remained passive?
Some sky calisthenics in secret employed?
  Or some perfect gymnast unheeding destroyed,
And invested me with the muscular treasure,
  Which gives to my labors an'exquisite pleasure?
So like to a gladiator sometimes I feel,
  That my brain with delirium almost will reel :
And I seem to behold the lords of brute force,
  As eager spectators who wildly lean out
From their cloud-amphitheatres, with many a shout
  And sign of delight, as I rage round the course.

For a nobler service I also am free :
  And the robing room of my masters I keep,
Where the ancient gowns of their order sleep :
  And often I see, or believe that I see,
What they lay aside as they come near me :
  What they take from their forms and give to the
      flower,
Hang on the neck of the swift-passing shower,
  Or fling o'er the wave-rent garb of the sea ;—
All brought from the farms of the far, solar plains,
  Where the quick, yellow seed is unweariedly sown,
And the harvests up-spring from the unburied grains,
  And at morning and evening are mown.

From their haunts and habits aerial,
  From the realms and regions imperial,

From their seats in the shade of the moon,
  Or on the white wings of the noon,
With greetings and grace magisterial,
  They come, when they hear the light fall
Of the seed, as their subtle recall.

Confused is the whir of their answering wings,
  And countless the gifts which every one brings ;
All poured in disorderly masses around,
  For Confusion still makes the first claim to the
    ground ;
But I am the foe of the mad Miscellaneous,
  And oppose with my weapons extemporaneous :
And I house like a shepherd the all holy Kinds,
  The images pure of infinite Minds.

But evil gets mixed with their glorious freight :
  As they sweep through the regions of far-spreading
    hate,
They catch from its seas the venomous drift,
  And defile in its froth the most sacred gift :
But I hear, as I list to them speeding along,
  How they heal it with blessings and purge it with song.

But alas ! how fateful and past their pure knowing,
  That their sacred touch is sometimes too glowing !
That the thrill of the heart and the speed of the thought,
  May oft on the earth-destined fabrics be wrought !
But I know, and I labor with might and with zeal,

To draw from the grain what makes the brain reel :
To draw from the fruit what shall blast with delight
  Since the bliss to the gods may to us be a blight ;
But strive as I may, they will never endure
  That a mortal shall sully what they have made pure.

Far different the harvest / take from my lords,—
  Ineffable motions and ravishing words ;
The *many* in *one* is revealed in each act,
  And multiplies ever each radiant fact ;
Each face I behold of that seraph band,
  Speaks the love of a legion, and each sacred hand
Thrills with the touch of the vibrating wire
  Which soweth the songs of some angelic choir ;
Each word is a poem, each sound a sweet song,
  And each blessing seems dropped from a glorified
    throng.

And learning of them, I interpret the world ;
  I see in each bud how the petals are curled ;
From each flying sound I loosen a trill ;
  From each drop of dew libations I spill ;
Each kernel of corn, which in foliage flows,
  Bears the ear on its currents with close topaz rows ;
All the least-valued things have their halos of glory,
  And the commonest word conveys a full story ;
Each star that revolves on its delicate cogs—
  Which ne'er with the load of its mysteries clogs —

Could people the sky with as splendid a host,
    If all who now roam there were hopelessly lost ;
Through the portal of *one* the *many* appear,
    And the many may bloom though the portal be sere ;
And the barren and dead into verdure will start,
When gathered by Love and sown on the heart.

THE MASON'S SONG.

When winds their stormy dredges dropped to earth,
    Deepening the channels of their furious flow :
And each cloud monster, round his mighty girth,
    Tightened his glittering girdle for a blow ;
There was a sound of many mortals falling,
    And solemn-voiced I heard the sad earth calling :

"My enemies prevail, my children die :
    Winds, rains, heat, cold, my armless breast attack :
And all the restless energies that fly,
    Grudging the peace which they must ever lack,
Murder the dear ones whom I love alone,
    And those who know my voice's large, low tone.

"O build me homes that evermore shall hold
    Those who come to me ! build me treasure-vaults,
Straight as the sun's sheer precipice of gold !
    Strong as the sky that ne'er its stars defaults !
Pure as the new moon's curving waterfall,
    That breaks in silvery mist illusional !"

The voice was pleading, yet its power such,
  That with the whirlwind's spiral draft,
Fell on my heart's calm atmosphere its touch,
  And drew it to the summit of my craft ;
This was my call as from a sacred tongue,
  And I became a mason while still young.

When first the scaffold's narrow ledge I walked,
  I seemed awakened to some old delight,
Vague and mysterious, which my senses balked,
  Yet dimly pictured to the inner sight ;
Sun, clouds, the winds and wingèd wanderers,
  Were to the steed beneath my heart as spurs.

But down I looked upon the grave, still earth,
  Whose solitude did seem to cover prayer ;
And, like a fertile loam, gave ready birth
  To quiet verdure which I found most fair ;
In vain sought winds to blow my love away ;
  Though it were dust, yet on my heart 'twould stay.

So to my wall I cleave and with it rise,
  Till I am higher than the trees ee'r clomb ;
Detect what they hold upward to the skies,
  And learn, besides, how keeps her crystal home
Each wingèd inmate of the airy spaces,
  Where nothing sullies and where naught defaces.

And I have builded many homes and fair ;
  Have often led my hollow squares of stone,

In many a charge against the foes of air,
  And conquered room to chamber peace alone ;
For if the space we win hold not repose,
  'Twere better that no place we should inclose.

Of every home, I love the most to build
  That one for which some loving pair shall wait--
In every other enterprise unskilled—
  To lead young Love within the unpassed gate :
But quite as sacred as where brides shall lie,
  Is where the good are born, and where they die.

But higher than my walls of brick or stone,
  I build light structures based upon my heart,
Reaching as high as ever bird hath flown,
  Bright as dissolven stars in every part ;
And rocking on the pulses of my days,
  Softly as shadows on the waterways.

Therein doth lie as in a wizard palace,
  A sweet, young spirit, sunk in charmèd sleep :
So lulled by craft of elemental malice,
  Since I refused to hear the winds that sweep :
But I shall kiss and cure that charmèd brow,
  When earth shall loose me from my early vow.

CONCLUSION.

  Thus sang they through the lessening light,
    And reared upon the pillared strain,
  To shield them from the growing night,
    The choral dome of a refrain ;

Which was not shaped o'er meager words,
   Nor ribbed by speech in any part ;
But bore aloft, like song of birds,
   The perfect arches of the heart.

So far was sped that fourfold song,
   So high that blended music went,
Each seemed precentor of a throng
   Of those whose song is never spent ;

But pours unwasting through the air,
   Through space unreached by other power ;
And aids the human voices rare,
   Which only holy Love doth dower.

Such might was in that singing band—
   Such might may perfect song display—
That though the night lay on the land,
   Where those men stood 'twas light as day.

I know not whence that light was shed—
   I only saw the quenchless glow—
Whether from some celestial head,
   That startling, luminous force did flow :

Or whether music's essence is
   A steady, white and limpid flame,
That fades whene'r it goes amiss,
   Through earthly hearts of darkened aim ;—

I know not, though I sometimes dream
  That loving hearts may keep the day :
And keep alive their fiery gleam,
  If long in music's draft they lay.

But in that light, where'er it sprung,
  I saw revealed a wondrous sight ;—
Before each heart of those who sung,
  Lay full displayed its secret might.

And far across the land there stretched
  The perfect product of each craft ;
As if the craftsman's dreams were etched
  Upon a mighty silver shaft.

Oh, earth and sea and man were dressed,
  As they were never dressed before !
Unless it were, when they expressed
  The life that leaped from every pore.

The ships that lived upon the sea,
  Seemed waves that broke not when up-cast :
The sails that with the winds agree,
  Were flowers that bloom upon the mast.

The fields before the farmers' feet,
  Had verdure that for e'er abides :
The harvests that the whole year greet,
  Were fattened in the solar tides.

The houses of the happy folk,
  Like living things, lay on the earth ;
And in chameleon changes spoke
  Each perfect moment's blissful birth,

And man again was nobly clad,
  In raiment equal to his face,
And every glowing member had
  A shield that hid no natural grace :

But matched the body's bright extern,
  And matched the throbbing life within ;
And veined for holy fires that burn
  All stains upon the tissue thin.

But as I watched those seraph forms,
  And lived as part of that bright scene,
A-sudden, night's black, locust swarms
  Began to fall on that pure sheen.

And as the snowy light grew dim,
  I knew the four-fold song was done ;
And in the twilight of that hymn,
  The parting of those men begun.

I could not see that sacred rite,
  Or know what parting words were said ;
But as they vanished from my sight,
  I heard faint moanings overhead.

THE TRAMP.

Some children played before me in the street,
  And, in my thought, they tripped o'er silver wires
Heart-fashioned of the past, and music sweet
  Rose from the stones in mists of rare desires ;—
When lo ! with shout of "Tramp !" they ran away,
To take elsewhere their never-alien play.

The tramp came slowly in the children's wake,
  As though he walked, with awe, on holy ground,
And in those empty realms of joy did shake,
  Aghast at having slain such happy sound.
"Come back !" he cried, "people again this place !
Come back, O Joy, with all thy radiant race !"

He nearer came, and I beheld him plain :
  A slender figure, finely wire-drawn,
As if to carry messages of pain ;—
  A face that seemed a quivering, white dawn :
And eyes like beacons on a dangerous coast,
That lighted but the ships already lost.

But coming near, he turned his eyes on me,
  And there appeared such largeness in his looks

As could not lie in self's small boundary ;
   And, like the sunfish in the sunny brooks,
Inquiry swam within those restless eyes,
And doubt upon them dropped her floating lies.

He paused and spoke to me, still standing there,
   With voice that sank before the feared reply,
And stranger words were never said, I swear !
   Since earth first shuddered at a human cry.
"I seek," he said, "what others do not need ;
If thou dost know its place, O thither lead !

"Far have I come, since I began the search ;
   My days seem strung, like beads, upon the way ;
And yet, I fear me, that beyond death's perch
   Must lie the goal for which I ever pray.
I know I have not passed it on the road,
For everywhere want's cry has been my goad.

"And ever have I questioned those I met,
   For tidings of the thing for which I sought ;
Have asked the laborer with his face of sweat,
   The idler in his dreams that come to nought ;
The old, beneath the shadow of their aims,
The young, who scarce are schooled in their joys' names."

"Enter," I said, "strange man, for rest and food,
   And tell me, after, all thy wondrous tale."
"The strong flow of my heart to Hunger's brood,

Sweeps food from mine own lips, as by a gale :
I am not weary, and my tale is brief ;
And thou shalt hear it for mine own relief.

" 'Twere better to be born on some bare rock,
    Or 'neath the clamorous cyclone's dervish feet ;
Or by the doors at which the lightnings knock,
    Or in the poisoned place where serpents meet ;
Than draw from Wealth's hot teat of blistering sand
Her dead-sea milk, by the sirocco fanned !

"Wealth is a fortress built against the sun ;
    An ambush set for angels : a defence
'Gainst the world's love ; an opiate cordial won,
    When Heaven's face would be the watcher's recom-
        pense ;
A draft from Styx ; a duct from that black stream
To irrigate the regions of a dream.

"I was born rich ; and all a father's gain
    Was stored away, with all the marks effaced
Of his strange instruments—once printed plain,
    And every purpose and result there traced ;—
The wealth was but a cavern home for me,
Beneath the sunny heights of industry.

"I lived as in a cave ; my treasure vaults
    Seemed filled by secret channels reaching up
To where creative labor never halts ;—

Seemed draining stealthily her humble cup :
The very drops upon my cavern wall
Were but the ooze of labor's pressing thrall.

"And when I sat without that dark recess,
    I saw the workmen passing to the heights,
With lowering brows and bodies comfortless,
    And hand that hardens slowly ere it smites ;
And bearing banners oft inscribed with "Want,"
Which they turned towards me with a frequent taunt.

"If down I traveled to the shaded deep,
    I found there but the ghost of the despoiled ;—
People whose names were whispered in my sleep,
    As having once upon my treasure toiled ;
Till I could find on every coin and stone
Some other's name ;—on none could see mine own.

"Oh, why is wealth established were it is,
    All toil above, and every want below ?
Why can it not be built in realms of bliss,
    Beyond the heights which toil doth crown like snow ?—
But yet, if it were there, 'twould fade in mist :
For in that holy air wealth never could exist.

"I had not learned to climb the lofty steep,
    And saw but horror in the vale below ;
I knew not where the vines of pleasure creep,
    Or where the summer draws her breezy bow

Across the silvery streamlet's tightened strings,
And through the viol of the pine tree sings.

"Oh, wealth is like a lonely, mateless bird,
    That dips it wings not in the common air !
Deep in the earth its heavy flight is heard,
    Where only it and reckless miners dare :—
What company for me in all the land,
When all around me had a different hand?

"I seemed a dam upon the streams of joy :
    A ligature upon a rounded vein ;
Or clot that might the baffled heart destroy,
    That it with life should never beat again :
Yet all that flowed before mine alien face,
Was marked for others in an other place.

"And why was I not *there?*   Why was I placed
    So near the fountain, that its forceful flow
Swept all things past ere ever I could taste ?—
    So near to Nature, that her mighty bow
Sent all her arrows far above my head,
And all her blessings far beyond me sped !

    "But I can *give*, I thought, if not *receive* :
    And I will draw my bow of generous deed,
And every arrow shall some want reprieve,
    Till one doth drop the thing which most I need :
And if it be what makes none other poor,
Then shall I take it, and it shall endure.

With eager hand I brought my treasures forth,
  And spread them in the sight of all who passed ;
What way soe'er they traveled, south or north
  Or east or west ; whatever greeting cast ;—
To each I offered what he most did crave ;
So long as one had want, I nought would save.

"When all was gone my weary quest began,
  To find, somewhere, the good none else did need :
And as I journey, everything I scan ;
  Nor doubt but that I shall at last succeed,
Although my way has ever been among
The things to which some private want was hung."

He turned away, and would not be restrained :
  I bowed my head, as if before a grave ;
For well I knew the land had ne'er contained,
  Nor ocean borne upon his highest wave,
The prize he sought ! but yet I knew, indeed,
He soon would find what others do not need.

DEMOCRACY.

Not on the crust of earth, Democracy,
Wert thou begotten ! but within the core
Of some fair, glowing world, all sea
And sunny motion to the boundless shore,
Whereto its balanced waves did sing and flow,
Poised blissful on its central unity :—
There wert thou born ; there didst thou freely grow,
Thou perfect infant, mothered by a world
Whose crowded lives, from every part,
Discharged their joys upon thine even heart :
And round its spheric longings curled,
That made thine earthward flight
Sweet things of sacred light.

Before man's foot had touched the earth's hard marge,
It had advanced its high, white peaks,
To make for thine a welcome large,
In sign of what it mutely seeks ;
And thou, as tender as a foam-child born
On Heaven's sea when surgeful Music speaks,
Or like the image on its bosom worn
When it is stilled to the star-pebbled shore,

By Peace who crosses with her muffled oar ;
Descended singing, but wert scarcely here,
Before thou seemedst a hardy mountaineer.

How in a moment wert thou changed !
Thy peaceful song became a battle cry,
Which from thee, somewhat, Love estranged ;
Thy sweetly ordered garb was turned awry ;
Its orbic emblems grew distorted,
As if by crossed attractions thwarted ;
The dust of strife soon blurred thy lustrous eye ;
Thy hands, unbalanced, moved confusedly ;
But thou didst falter not ; thy heart was whole,
And had no flaw for fear to nestle in ;
And dauntlessly thou strodest towards the goal,
Which still was shining through the dusty din
Where man should settle from some shattered sphere,
With splinters buried in his heart of fear.

Brief was thy waiting ; since thou scarce hadst taught
The earth to graft with silvery streams her seas,
And scarce the forest's friendly compacts wrought,
And grouped all living things in families ;
When man fell startled on the earth's hard rind,
With vision shaken from its central seat,
And henceforth to his spirit's marge confined,
As he to earth's, and margined things to greet ;
And ever out from his own glory turned,.

As his new shadow from the sun was spurned.
And while bewildered and afraid he lay,
He saw aloft a hateful bird of prey,
That, like an auger, bored with spiral wings
The clear air towards him and his sweet heart-springs ;
And from the clouds he heard the houseless thunder,
And wild beasts raging in the forest under ;
But Nature's quiet explanations made
With song of bird and sunlight's aid,
And flowers stationed just beyond the shade,
He knew not, since he was not brave ;
For Beauty even shuns a slave.

Art thou unmoved, Democracy?
So listlessly thou movest toward the spot.
Has the cold strangled thy divinity,
Or heat engaged in some malicious plot,
To foil thy fleetness? or, in sudden freak,
Hast thou the swift wind chased, that now so weak?
But lo ! I wronged thee, since thy glorious face,
Of earthly weariness reveals no trace ;
But there before thee in the untried way,
Rise foes whose strength is little less than thine ;
Who claim o'er man the first delusive sway ;
And must oppose thee and thy thoughts divine.
There stand Oppression, Hatred, Ignorance,
And Fear, the phantom, with his looks askance ;
But on thy face one only image lies :

'Tis that of Pity writing thy resolve ;
And thou dost look in longing toward the skies,
To find the spot where shall again revolve
Man's golden world, with man himself restored—
His lordly head no longer lowered.

Hark ! does that sacred vision turn to song?
O holy Pythoness, was that a chant,
Which from thy laughing lips rose up so strong,
That Tumult's tangle were a breaker scant
For that full flood, which could not be confined
By aught save music of a nobler kind?
Like seraphs' songs heard round their perfect spheres,
The wild strain flows ! Earth's captured hills
No more keep guard ! the lightning's broken spears
Strike down the airy powers of hostile wills !
The free winds aid, and scornfully reject
All other messages ; but thine protect,
Until they strike the ears of men enslaved,
And turn again to vision ! Men are saved !

And now, thy foes eluded, I behold
Thee mingling watchfully among men :
Confusion follows on thy footsteps bold ;
And thou dost smite the despot, Order, when
He only ranges men in graded rows,
To walk in single file and not oppose
The mandate of the foremost man in line.
And thou dost tell men not to look on *one* ;

But turn their eyes where'er the sun doth shine
To show a man ; or where there now is none,
If only once his shadow there has lain.
And thou dost show that fear's the only stain
Which cannot be washed off of human hands ;
That man's full soul hath room for no commands ;
And that his brow had not been left so bare,
If but Subjection's name were to be printed there.

Where hast thou learned that look of wrathful scorn?
Hast thou seen brawls aforetime among gods?
Or Heaven desecrated, when some demon-born
Intruder, smites the seraph he defrauds
Of his exalted rights? Or hast thou seen
An aweless seraph do some common task,
Nor raise his eyes when near him gods unmask,
And leave unbared their glory-shedding mien?
For when thou seest man sordid, cheating, raging,
And chiefly, when before thee, man strikes man,
Thy features show no longer mercy's plan ;
But mark a passion that is long assuaging ;
But when thou seest a man erect
A paltry structure which he calls a throne,
For his lone seat, and calmly doth expect
Mankind to be its base of lifeless stone ;
Then laughter loosens but thy light contempt,
At what from serious care is well exempt ;
Thy hand but rises and the thing is gone.

Thou speakest not to all ; but first dost choose
Thy trusty confidants ; men of reserve,
Of hearts world-modeled, and of thews
That might have bent a mountain to its curve,
Yet would have feared to crook or cramp
The slender column of another's will,
First raised to hold the inspired lamp
Of consecrated thought in mists of ill.
To them thou needest no interpreter :
For thou dost ever speak their ancient speech,
Which they have learned where deities confer,
And still doth echo in the soul of each.
How dost thou tutor these, thine own elect?
What grace bestow from thine abundant store?
Dost thou their hardened limbs with charms protect,
Or on their eyelids dreamy lotions pour?
Nay ! thou dost simply show that one free soul
Out-weighs the whole of Nature's beady bowl,
If base submission mixes with the drink ;
And teachest these devoted ones to think
It good to perish for their cowering race,
And crowd their boundless lives into a moment's space.

Is Death's thy service then? didst thou appear
To only show the mortal how to die,
And from his latest, living thought to rear
The standard of a dim eternity?—
To leap at one strong bound all life's extent,

And dwell one fiery moment on its verge,
And then spring lightly to his banishment
Into the dark abyss—the unseen surge—
And holding in his hands upraised,
A little snow snatched from life's highest peaks,
Or winter rose by icy breezes glazed,
To charm away the demon vulture-beaks?—
This is thy mission then? Nay, never so !
But the free spirit housed in every man,
Thou wouldst, full-statured and resistless, show
To feeble thousands who could never scan
Its noble image in their shrunken thought,
Nor use the powers to their fingers brought.

But in the splendor of a great man's death,
The darkened places of the mind are light ;
And with the flutter of his latest breath,
The earth is shaken by a thing of might :
And the world-currents which were lately choked,
Break down all dams which selfish strength hath made,
Or wrongful purpose hath invoked
To stop the stream of Nature's equal aid :
And in the quiet of the afterflow,
Thy voice is heard again ; and thou dost teach
That Nature is distrustful, and doth countermand
Each perfect gift, unless the whole shall reach
The destined port of every empty hand ;
That though a man may rise to his full height,

To lend her momentary aid, she knows
To put him straightway from material sight,
Till man no longer shall a man oppose ;
That there's no sceptre save the unclogged arm,
Nor any crown but that which fits all heads
With equal grace—reflects to none a harm,
But glory of enfranchised eyes instead,
And bounds dominion by its circling line ;
That Freedom is the light of the Divine,
The soul's true gladness and its starry glow :
That man should *pause*, if Freedom may not *go* ;—
Should scorn a seat, though gods should pass the place,
If he might not be free to turn away his face.

Yet, O thou godess, one ignoble art
Thou teachest ! for thou goest among those
Who gather up the overflow of Nature's heart ;
Who watch whene'er the careless hands unclose,
And drop their holdings ; and who stealthy catch,
With ready basins and expert dispatch,
The very drops which fall from lips that praise
The sweet elixirs of laborious days :
To such, and to the ones who save with greed,
The flying atoms from the sharpening blade
Of effort 'gainst the whirling stone of need,
Thou sayest a thrifty word, and givest aid
To count and to divide the shameful gains :—
Oh ! show not thy white fingers lasting stains?
Better, O stooping one, hadst thou, instead,

Called up a flood at close of every day,
Wakened a whirlwind from its spiral bed,
And washed and blown the stained hoard away !

O Democracy, reclaim this erring crowd !
Show thyself to them in thy pristine might !
Unfold the grace wherewith thou art endowed ;
Raise thy majestic form to its full height !
Set straight thy struggle-torn, disorded dress !
Take up the symbol of a human heart
Carven from gold and purged of its distress,
Which lies upon the ground there where thou art,
And very near thy feet !   Sing thou again !
O sing of Joy and Truth and Love ! explain,
That joy is like a sea whose tides do dash
On the broad beaches of a race, and not
On capes of favored beings crash !
O take from off man's heart Fear's fingers hot,
And turn its tremors to the pleasant thrill
Of music ! Show, that though Joy counteth hearts,
Whene'er she opens her fine treasuries,
Nature, more wary, counts but honest hands,
Ere she permits the lessened gifts to pass :
And say or sing where Nature doth conceal
The gathered glories of fecundate time,
Which she ordaineth never to reveal,
Till all men gather in some gentle clime :
And round the spot a perfect circle shape,
Lest one small gap should let the whole escape !

THE SUBJECT SPIRIT.

A spirit was captured when Love kept guard
  On the marge of her fair free world alone,
And the secret pass was left unbarred
  Which led where the seat of her empire shone.

The fetters were fixed ere she was aware,
  While the rare sweet song on her lips fell dead,
And fancies of wondrous flights in air
  Sank in the deeps of her heart like lead.

All the symbols of self were snatched away,
  With the wonderful things her hands had wrought
In the fading sheen of each passing day
  To the beauteous mould of her easy thought.

From her form was taken her delicate dress,
  Which but bodied the glow of her inward grace,
And the only screen to her dumb distress
  Was the common garb of a servile race.

And her captors in haste conveyed her far,
  To a place where gloomiest vapors roll,
Where her home was built 'neath a baleful star,
  Under the arch of a single soul.

'Twas a wondrous dwelling of substance fine,
　Of a changeful form and a fickle hue,
With as many rooms in its strange design
　As the heart has places for pleasures new.

But the house was empty except for *one*
　And the shadows which his choked heart did spill :
For the structure was built by his hands alone,
　And was girded around by his single will.

And this ghostly house where she dimly dwelt
　With the lord she served with abasèd head,
Would dilate with the leave of its magic belt,
　Or shrink to the smallest space instead.

But expand or diminish, however it might,
　The bounds of her slavery never were crossed ;
And the sway of another to her seemed right,
　Since the way of a separate life was lost.

Oh ! a piteous sight was this helpless slave,
　As she flitted about in an aimless way ;
But only advanced where her master drave,
　And only remained where he bid her stay.

Yea ! her hand in the wake of his own hand moved,
　And her deed was his doing, while ever his need
But her own need unto her dim thought proved,
　And her pain with his own pain fully agreed.

Her voice only filled the old mould of his speech,
 And the dross in the draught of his eyes,
Alone fed the eyes the blank days did leech
 With the drouthy lips of a false sunrise.

If alone she was left with her phantom household,
 While he flung his glad heart 'gainst the upper-
  most sky,
With a wild, free wing and a joy untold,
 Her own wings quivered she scarce knew why.

His exhausted emotions revived in her heart,
 And she fondly believed her own heart was alive ;
And the music that from his tense being did start,
 To repeat on slack strings she did strive.

There is such a delight in a soul's free play,
 That one is not sad who can merely repeat
The motions that picture that consummate way,
 And the mere imitation seems wondrously sweet ;

Just as if some imperial flower should grow,
 Whose shadow itself was a dim, dusky bloom,
And sent from the wells of its half-smothered glow
 The delicate hint of a subtle perfume.

Now had passed a long time since a prisoner came
 This weak, wronged soul to her prison-house wierd,
And she lovlier grew notwithstanding her shame,
 And unto her liege more and more was endeared.

For 'tis easy to love what resideth so nigh
  To the love-beating heart, that its echoes return
The loud stroke of self with each lover-sweet cry
  Which leaps from the heart which has self yet to
    learn

His love was as sure her own love to find,
  As the rainbow is sure to come up with the rain,
For it bowed but the mists of his masterful mind,
  And its hues were entwined like the links of a
    chain.

But the world-heart true has a world-old cure
  For a heart enslaved and a heart that sways,
And the time soon comes when it will not endure
  That a lie shall discolor the deeps of the days.

Then she sends her tides which are christened death :
  The white, keen tides which dissolve all deceit,
And turn to the stuff of the lightest breath
  The bonds that her truth and her love defeat.

And these tides arose on this mateless pair,
  And the shadows shrank and the falsehoods fell,
Till between the flood and the crystal air
  Were two naked souls and a broken spell.

Then at first, like to two leashed darts, they fly
  Straight up from that silent and waveless waste,

And the ether new sang a sweet reply
  To the rhythmic beat of their wings of haste.

For a million of leagues ever forward they flew,
  But no place of repose did they anywhere find,
And fatigued near to fainting then both souls grew,
  But especially she of so gentle a mind.

Now a flash ! and a new world lies in their sight ;
  The spontaneous child of immaculate stuff
So refined, that to quicken it into the light,
  The percussion of angelic wings is enough.

The purgèd air might have given it birth,
  For 'twas light as the foam which the waves dis-
    perse,
And embodied the grace of the rarefied worth
  Which, diffused, doth fecundate the universe.

Quickly thither, aweary, the fugitives turned,
  With their long-lonely hearts newly peopled with
    hopes,
And their eyes some ineffable essences burned
  That escaped from the sheen of that world's won-
    drous slopes.

All at once, there was woe for that voyaging twain;
  In their faces the force of a sudden storm blew ;
And it rose to a blast, and their struggles were vain,
  For the new world bade them to wander anew.

And apart, and as dead, they were carried away.
By the winds that sprung from that tenantless world,
With their sad, shining wings all in disarray,
    And their white breasts up, they were therefrom
    whirled ;

And were left to drift in the vast unknown,
    Past the drifting moon or a fixèd star,
Till received on some sphere of a lower zone,
    They might live again in that world afar.

THE WHOLE TRUTH.

"For Anthony, my husband," was inscribed
The packet found upon the woman's breast,
When women came in prompt apprenticeship
Of death, to dress her fitly for the grave ;
And, underneath, was added, "To be read
At once, and placed again where it was found."
Within, the wretched man first read these lines ;
"O blameless man, true friend, wise counsellor,
Look once upon the face that thou has loved,
After the truth is known, and in the white,
Soft splendor of thy heart's benignity,
Let the dark flake of this my secret sin
Be melted and consumed ; or if thou must,
Still yet recall from that white, helpless face
All the fond, faithful looks which thou has let
The lie there snare from thee, lest there remain
Some little spot not false, some slightest trace
Of olden smile upon it, to front God with.
Thou thoughtest not when thou assuringly
Didst kiss the last breath forth from these weak lips—
For so I see my life shall pass away—
That thou didst sow a seed in that black ground,

From which should spring such bitter, blighting words
As are here writ. But nay ! it is not so ;
Though I being dead yet speak, I speak not now
With lips that have learned phrases or bestowed
Translations of the heart's black-letter past
To false impression of new happiness ;
But I do now announce the very *soul*,
As one deprived of every earthly thing,
And standing in the single element
Of higher worlds where nothing doth exist
Whereby a falsehood may be signified."

Here followed a long space unwritten on,
As though she fain would let his fancy build
A gradual stairway of his rising dread
Unto the awful heights of her next words.
The following sheet began abruptly thus :
"Love is a ball of shrouded fire let down
Invisibly between love's candidates ;
Thy subtle instincts only gave thee power
To draw the covering from the side towards me,
So that dark-lanternwise, it only shone
Upon my heart, and left thine own obscure.
Thou couldst but sing the morning song of love :—
The sun rose later.   Thou couldst early wake
Love's angel tented o'er the quiet heart,
But she did waken *blind*, and did mistake
Thy hand for that of her true mate, until

One came who touched her eyes to sight.
I have not truly loved thee any time ;
That which we thought was love has only been
The soul's rise to the gauge of custom, not
The tide profound that drowns material things.
Yet in these days of doubt and weariness,
Seeing thy goodness round me everywhere,
Sometimes I almost have believed that love
Showed not within the white light of thy life,
Because, star-like, it could be seen to shine
But in the evening of a darker nature.

After our marriage there was calm accord,
Sweet fellowship and even happiness ;
For happiness doth build on level floors
Of such concomitance, and not on slopes
Of superposed or far-receding aims.
And in this wise two quiet years passed by,
Like white swans on a quiet stream ; the third—
That was a white swan too, but wondrously
Sheeted with bleachen flame, and thrilling all
The upper air with daring feats of flight,
Until it seemed it must have surely found,
In that etherial world of buoyancy,
Some upward-flowing stream of blessedness,
And on its mounting currents of delight,
Followed its shadow heavenward ; for *that year*
Came he of whom I now must truly write.

A spirit with a strange and potent spell,
That may be used but once ; a deity
Who shows his ichor-veinèd breast, his arms
Force-tissued out of lights incomparable,
And world-empictured palms to one marked soul ;—
That is a lover, when that common word
Slips from its rags of use and shows pure flesh.
"Tis one that shows the old divinity
Is stronger than the new humanity.
Such seems me that I had.   When first he stood
Inside the room where I sat silently,
It seemed he was a messenger for me ;
And I felt wronged when he looked not my way,
But spoke to others unconcernedly.
Yet, as he talked, the fairy oars of speech
Sent subtle ripples through the sea of sound
To my ears only—music's mysteries
And fine, delicious sympathies.
Later, when he first spoke to me, it seemed
There was a sudden light turned on, and through
The cavern world, wherein I long had lived,
Went myriads of sprites along the walls,
Waking embedded gems ; while I thought speech
Had ne'er before been put to such a use,
But like some strange utensil of the gods,
Left carelessly on earth, grotesquely false
Had been men's doubtful, childish touch, until
The wonder fell into his hands, and now,—
The true intent—right touch, and thus
The miracle.

I will not try to trace
The days that followed, nor make visible
The different beauty of each passing face ;
Let this be all ; with song and seraph voice
Each did announce to my enraptured heart
The new force thrilling through the universe.
Either the world sank round it, or my soul
Rose lightened of some coarser element ;
I felt as though some secret agency
Was working 'gainst the earth's attractive power ;
The sun and stars seemed forcibly to draw me ;
The light, free winds and wonders of the air
Did make me of their moving company.
Before, I had enjoyed some little things I had
Close pressed against my claim-declaring heart ;
But *now* was all diffused and wholly free,
Yet was the whole enjoyed unceasingly ;
And day became all sunrise, and the night
Was daylight starred.

There was a strong soul near
To hold mine own, invincibly, against
The void around, wherein the single soul,
Unless so hedged, is ofttimes dissipate.
Here was the one thing I so oft had lacked ;—
The close quicksilver to the pure glass
Of being, making it a mirror which
Reveals that coy and covert wonder, *Self.*

Blame not o'ermuch, if in this vivid life
Of our two spirits, so precisely set
In correspondence that each lightest thought
Was echoed back in happy emphasis,
That the plain utterance and attributes
Of others not so surely re-inforced,
Should be but faintly felt and soon effaced.

But slowly did a change grow manifest ;—
A change so fine, impalpable indeed,
That twilight's rare and subtly-moving mists
Could scarce have noted it by sorcery.
Would a cloud's shadow weight a swallow's wing,
And make a serious accident of flight ?—
So little was our coming ill first felt.
It must be that some faculty of love
Is baffled in our mortal atmosphere,
Ere Imitation can find any room
To set her earthly mirrors in, and fling
Into the mingled lucence of two souls,
Dim, haunting shadows of the incomplete ;—
Hints of the human, common, fallible,
And maddening phantoms of the world's wild way.
The bond was not so close that foreigners
Crossed not the boundaries of our crystal world,
But rather were brought in, because of want
In our own fairy populace ; while *these*
Were driven forth.   It seemed my lover now

Was not content with all our love had stored
In secret, in the heart's pure cabinets,
But did require the meaner pleasure, too,
Of boldly spending all again.   But this
I saw not then, nor truly did he see.
One day you left me unexpectedly ;
And when he came again, a different look
He gave me, and his face was strangely changed ;
No more his looks did join themselves to mine,
That both might turn in double power toward Heaven,
But they opposed them,—stopped abruptly there,
As though their faulty aim was fully reached.
His glowing eyes seemed set in emptiness—
So great the longing in them, and his face
Did pale and slowly unto whiteness turn,
As though the soul's white light must gradually
Be all transferred to it, before he dared
To speak the new word growing in the lips.

And thus the word was spoke : one day he came
And stood long time in silence by my side,
Then forced the fierce words forth unwarningly :
'*He* has the *whole* of life, give me *one day.*"
I rose and stood away, but instantly
He fell upon his knees in front of me,
Crying "One day ! one day ! one day !"   But I
Would hear no more, and ran from him in fear ;
And hid myself; and saw him not for days.

But ever was I closely canopied
With echo of that sad conjuring cry :
Yea ! it was writ upon the walls, and lay
Upon the floor to thrill my very feet
Whene'er I walked.   Some wizard wall did shut
This one thought from all other thoughts, until
It seemed a burning island in a mental waste,
And only *one* could build the saving mole,
To bind it back unto the continent
Of universal thought and sanity ;
And *he* was ever at my door in wait.

But quickly will I tell the rest that fell ;
Disguised I met him e'er the day was near,
And rode afar, before the glowing moon
Had coyly put her morning wimple on :—
Rode swiftly down the eastern slopes of night
And up the grand crescendo of the dawn,
Until we reached an unknown wood, and there
Upon its margin did await the day.
Then spoke he, and his sweet, expressive eyes
Did seem to follow all his forceful words
To my heart's door, as might, in sooth, attend
Some holy handmaids on divinity.
'For this one day,' he said, 'I would that thou
Shouldst love me only and exclusively,
Until all other loves, all other men,
The world itself to misty softness turn,

Becoming but the unseen fragrance shed
From out the visible, red rose of love.
Then I will show thee my heart openly,
And I will teach thee, sweet, to reconstruct
The world in quivering forms of its own longings.'
Then as the sun was rising, tenderly,
With smiles he mooted where the day began ;
Whether the place might be the upper rim
Of the sun, or lower ; whether her first flight
Was over or beneath that burning sphere ;—
One doubting moment—then we faced the wood.

At midday, looking through the trees, he said,
'See how the sun doth aid the stooping day,
Lifting the arches of her crystal cave,
That, standing at full height, her haloed head
May touch the mark of noon.' At night he said,
Watching the sun go down, 'See, as he sinks,
That quick, black dragon of the sea of night
Leaps upward fiercely to his drooping breast.'
And speaking so, his last kiss likewise sank
Below the flushed horizon of my lips,
Which nevermore in all my life should glow
With passage of those burning spheres of love,
Sun-risen in his heart, sun-set in mine.
I saw not that they soon should rise again,
Ejected from the sickened heart, and stained
With its red blood, like dreadful portents, cross

The dull, bare skies of hateful after-days,
In cruel iteration of my sin.

    What need to speak of the return?   What need
To speak his name? he named himself anew
For that one day, and swore his old name was not fit
To mate with such a joy ; and called the new
To Heaven, that in the first amaze of death
He might be greeted by it, and so called forever.

    Being at home, at first there was no change in me ;
You came not back, my lover came not near.
The life within, still heavy and o'ercharged
With dangerous chemic fulminants which gave
Explosive splendor to it, still controlled,
As stronger than the steady light outside.
That lawless, daring day, too large at first,
Dilated with the growth of time, until
It seemed 'twould ever dome the temple built
Of common days, and through its riot-wrought
And crystal-prisoned hues and traceries,
Give colors and delicious light to life.
But 'twas a day misplaced and overstrained
With burden of too strong significance.
One day alone, can crown the whole of life,
And that, the last, which Death shall hold for us,
And help us work our final fancies on.

    My lover came not near, and it grew hard
To hold that magic vault of interwoven joys

Above the single pillar of my heart,
The other fair and fellow column gone.
Each morning was the waxing of a hope,
Each night its withering ; the full world shrank
Around my spirit's sad impoverishment ;
The sun rose dwarfed above the lowered hills,
For want of him, and every sweet of day
Was lessened by the absence of his face ;
And everything in Nature's catalogue
Of dear, delicious beauties, seemed to bear
A broad, black scar, where erst, incorporate,
The increase of his radiant image lay.
Dimmer the world grew ; now, no more the light
Was strong enough to show the finest shapes
Hiding behind the garments of the visible ;
And those fair phantoms of imagined glory,
Created by the double working force
Of interblending spirits, now recoiled
And faded in the far, unfollowed glooms.
The earth was at my door ! and he who first
Had closed the golden bolt, had gone away
And left the fatal door unbarred, and me
Defenceless from the rough intruder there.

Sometimes I would not watch, remembering
How unannounced he first stood at my side ;
And fancying that, soothly, even now
He was endeavoring to reconstruct

That lone and devious highway of surprise
Between the hedges of my close-set looks,
Which he had laid before unto the marge
Of my unwatchfulness.   Nay, then 'twould seem
That only in the common, open avenues,
Could he again come near me ; all the world
Had been transfused with our wild, burning love,
And there no more remained the unseen things,—
Illusive beauty, dear obscurity,
And shy, veiled essence of delightfulness,
To work surprise with, but with bold acclaim
Of every sentient thing and rabble cry
Of guilty memories, would his approach
Be coarsely heralded.

                    And then I knew
He would not come again ; that he would wait,
Till in the fine and stainless elements
Of some new world, he'd work that wonder o'er
And find me subtly-conscious, yet surprised.
And then a new mood mastered me, and gave
A new sign unto my clairvoyant heart.
He would not come again ; he therefore must
Be going farther from me every hour ;
And all this ebb of light and splendrous life,
Was but his footstep far within the dark.
How, what our two souls had made right, was now
A growing guilt to my unaided soul,

And could not be enforced to radiancy
By its lone light !   Oh, how inexorably
Condensed in pain and resolidified
The actual world to old familiar shapes,
Which had dissolved and been etherialized
In our love's fervency !   How far from me
Must he have traveled certainly, to make
Those mountains take again material ways !
How far, before that bare field, half way down
Their pliant side, seemed not the open page
Of some Titanic register, wherein
All floating wonders of the air inscribed
Their names, in passing, but again became
The highest record of the tide of toil !
How far, before that highway 'cross the vale
Let pass dim memories of the common flood
That flowed there ere his coming struck away
All footprints save his own, and lifted up
A purged way towards the heavens !   But how far,
How very far, was he before the walls
Of my own room unveiled the pictured things
Upon them, and revealed, close to my eyes,
Your portrait hanging there with life in it !

You tell me I was sick when you came home,
And that which followed, from the hour I saw
Your face come back unhindered to the wall,
Was but the natural sequence of the shock

Which flung the eerie flambeaux of the mind,
From their precise adjustment with the sight
Confusedly upon it.   Yet, how small
The exposition for so vast a fact !
No ! No ! for those few weeks of earthly time
My soul was recommitted to the elements,
And lived out eons of majestic suffering.
Ages I lay beside a stream of fire,
With both stained hands plunged in to burn them pure ;
For centuries, my lips did spout hot springs,
And still remained unclean ; for longer time
Than earth's most lengthened records mark,
I groped through gloomy space, in wild, waste search
For something nameless but imperative ;
And every star I neared grew dark and sank
As though it were a stone, till I would rend
My breast, and with my frenzied fingers
Tear away the coverings of my outraged heart,—
To let a black stream forth which only drained
An ever-filling sin, and poured its fatal tide
'Cross countless leagues of sky immaculate,
To mingle with the Milky Way and turn
Its lustrous currents to another Styx.
At last, upon some dread and desolate strand,
Amid the wrecks of stars and dreary drift
Of noble enterprises cast 'gainst spite,
It seemed that I did die or fall asleep ;
The next I knew, was you beside my bed,
Physician-like, with fingers on my pulse.

How curiously I watched you those first days !
I could not understand your look of youth ;
Nor why you kept attendance at my side.
Why was your hair not white—as mine must be—
And face all written o'er in age's script
By age's shaking hand? Why had you still
A memory of her who slipped away
So long ago? That clock upon the wall,
Whose tick was still so fresh,—had it in truth,
For all these years been breaking stony time
Upon the highway of corporeal change,
And still worked on unworn? It could not be !
But it and you and every earthly thing
Had stopped, and waited till my swift race ceased.

Then all that had been e'er my race began,
My perfidy, dishonor and despair ;
All which that weary flight through space
Had borne me farther from, was *new* to you ;—
Was even yet so new, perhaps the mind
Had not sent judgment to the waiting hand ;
Nay, why not e'en so new that no account
Had yet been carried to the judging mind?
Oh, fatal power of thought ! only to see
The *new* in you did make the *new* in me ;
And on the apex of the stalk of pain
My sin's red flower bloomed out suddenly.
A sudden tumult in the brain—Hope's touch—

Fear's evil sorcery ; or simply there
Was just uncovered by that passing flood
Some hidden force imbedded in the mind ;
When lo !   there lay a thing unseen before :
'Twas new deceit ; I seized it and deceived.

    First thought I of that magic room which you
Had left me guardian of while you were gone,—
The chamber of our coupled lives, enriched
With joint creations of converging minds ;
Now, like a hollow shell, it lay despoiled
Upon that shore from which love ebbed away,
Holding but ghostly murmurs of the past.
How quickly I invented counterfeits,
To garnish over those weird, empty walls !
Afraid, that by some subtly-knowing smile,
Some reminiscent look or secret word,
You might make quick demand of my false heart,
To show some bauble of the scattered charge.
How cunningly I strove to cheat your eyes,
And baffle all the cunning of the heart,
By my assumptions and false attitudes !
Oft-times I would clothe common things in Love's
Habiliments ; say, 'This and this is Love,
And thus have I seen Love look many times ; '
Maligning Love with false resemblances,
Lest you might really know how fair she was,
And what a false pretender then was I.

From then to now my aim has been to dupe—
To break the truth and shape the parts to lies ;
But every lie that showed smooth face to you,
Did have a sharp side pressed against my heart.
Say, 'twas not all in vain ! say that from out
Those black and biting mists of noxious thought,
One pure drop of joy was yet distilled,
To give you just one moment's blessedness ;—
And I will swear each lie was very good,
And Heaven shall hold it e'en as righteousness !

But what shall I say *there* about my sin,—
The love, and that whereto it lead ?   The love,—
That was of God ; the error comprehends
The form it took.   The common, human mould ;—
Who has prepared it and concealed the thing
Under illusion and the subtle net
Of mystic longings towards the infinite ?
I own not that I loved my love too much ;
My fault was that I loved him not enough ;
Our neighboring spirits could not quite burn through
The barriers of coarse, earthly habitude ;
And through the charred and shapeless aperture,
Caught only broken views and fickle fallacies
Of sight, in place of fullest revelation
Of each immortal countenance, with all
Its true, divine expression unmistakable.
A little more of love,—he would have seen

Your shadow on my face : he would have seen
Mine eyes had been indentured unto thine
To give them joy : he had not failed to know
That all the twice-enkindled and abounding light,
Wherein our hearts did lie, like ruby sprites
That bathe in floods of bleachen pearl, should fall
On thee for yet a little time, until
Thy heart did feel the double love in it,
And be advised thus, soon and painlessly,
Of that full life of highest excellence
Which we had found without thy heart's consent,
Or contribution of its slightest beat,
But yet was drained of its supremest joys
To pay a wrongful tribute to thee.   Then
Thou hadst been fortified against the loss
Of faulty fellowship, by seeing rise
The luminous shadow of the needed one
Thou wouldst go search for.

       Pardon me, lone man,
That I have been but only pity's shade
Beside thy loneliness ! give me this praise,
That there was grief within my grief, because
Your heart did topple like a leaning tower,
Being unpropped by other, fellow heart !
God will not blame me that I could not love,
But that, what time I loved, my radiant love
Did not so beat on thee, and thee illume,

That the fine lines of my enscriptured pledge
Had not grown dim or obsolete, until
The rightful sanction of thine own free choice,
And magic of the moving truth in thee,
Did brush it off.   Had I not done thee wrong,
How easily ! I might have taught thee this ;
Had I not shadowed thee with shame,
How soon ! thou wouldst have learned it for thyself.

Pardon me now, for truth's sake, though the truth
Is bitter, being over-kept within
The airless damps of my long reticence,
And at the last, mayhap, is told amiss !
Pardon me now, for love's sake, though my love
Was hatred to thine honor for a day !
Be not too wroth, nor suffer over much,
Lest fear shall make me falter before God !"

Here ceased the writing, but the reader ceased
Not yet his weeping, though he many times
Did kiss the sheet with tender reverence,
And murmured brokenly, "Poor penitent,
Thy pardon is already five years old,
And was dispatched to Heaven the very hour
I heard the story from thy raving lips ;
Be thou assured ! Too much have I been blessed
Having the time-touch of so fine a hand as thine !"

LOVE IN THE LIGHT.

O Love, stand forth from the midst of the others,
   Who are mimicking thee with irreverent eyes,
And the shadow-gloom of whose hinderance smothers
   The light that of right on thy sweet face lies.

But vermilion the cumbrous shadow of one is,
   And it heavily droops till it lies in thy way ;
And it clasps thee low down as at earliest sunrise
   The low-kneeling Dawn clasps the white knees of Day.

Is it true, as they say, that the drift of the spirit
   Has heaped thy white breasts like the sands on the
      beach,
When the hot land-winds blow o'er it and sear it ?
   Do the bones of our heart's dead lie there and bleach ?

Nay, rather declare, as thy smiling avouches,
   They are sacred guests of thine innocency,
Who are resting in peace on their ivory couches ;—
   There are three of you now whom I see.

Thine eyes are not domes of the impious temples
  Whose altars with sinfulest sacrifice reek ;
But, instead, they are only the sweetest examples
  Of holiest height and sun-pointed peak,

Where the fearless explorer easily rallies
  The fairy-like train of his soul's retinue,
That has lingered too long in the slumberous valleys,
  Where the foliage droops with a sweet-scented dew.

Like ripples of wine in an over-filled beaker
  Are thy lips that revive all that sickens in me ;
Not as quicksands are they to the Infinite-seeker
  Who is lured by the pink shells cast from the sea.

Thy brow doth resemble the far, west horizon
  When the sun has left nought but his breath in the air,
While another sun lays his etherial dyes on
  The changeable mists interfusing thy hair.

How thy breath doth dissolve, like a sky-filtered ether,
  The smoke-breath of Passion still near to thy feet !
Which is thick from the fires which mortals bequeath her,
  When they die with their heart's flame still incomplete.

Oh, how animate ! art thou though thou art standing,
  And my slow heart exulteth to keep pace with thee,

As thou trainest my feet to obey thy commanding,
  And old Lethargy taketh his mantle from me.

Elixirs do flow in the founts of thy being :
  And thy heart is the sheath of a delicate star,
Which distilled fire's essence ever is freeing,
  And beating to concurrent galaxies far.

How divine is thy power ! which so easily foileth
  The art of thy foes and pain's sharpest pangs ;
And when round us the Night like a black serpent coileth,
  With what cunning of hand thou drawest the fangs !

And his scaly skin thy magic art turneth,
  By an instant touch, to the swan's neck of Day,
Where supernal joy its white light ever burneth,
  Till it seemeth the curve of a heavenly way.

Of all who have visited us from a far sphere,
  Thou alone doth retain thy natural dress ;
And bringest the glow of thy untarnished star-gear,
  Which loseth no light in the dark of distress.

For thou only couldst carry beauty's vast burden
  Through the measureless flight and the infinite space,
Till thou gainest a world for thy unequalled guerdon,
  And givest an infinite joy to a race.

And thou art become our world's guide and pathfinder ;
And the golden spade of thy office is held
In thy firm right hand, as a faithful reminder
Of the highways unbuilt and the regions unquelled.

But an errorless map of the heart-country pathless,
Thou dost hold in thy left hand close to thy breast ;
And through desert or jungle thou travelest scathless
To the heart that faints for thy gentle behest.

But lo, thou art gone ; yet, again, I have found thee !
And thy shadow I see upon Death's darkened wall !
And I hear the soft leaves as they rustle around thee,
From the other side where thy singing doth call.

THE LOST CLUE.

Can sound be linked to sunbeams? or the hearts
Of men be tethered to a god's desire?
Surely, some god hath passed too near, and I
Must ever follow, charmed and dreamily,
As in his wake the drafted stars might roll.
Or is this thought a mask of madness only?
May it not be a phosphorescent film
Over the shallow sea whereon I float,
Hiding the hideous monsters of my brain's
Profound disease, until they are full grown?
What man before, so daring that he scorned
The pole-star's fixed and servile indicator?
Denied that there was north or south or east
Or west to human destiny, but made
His life the flaming center of a bold
And radiant purpose, which insphered in light
All human kind?

       The lily of my hope,
It seems, had risen high above its root,
And spread the petals of its vast intent
Upon the waters of some life divine :

My thought has been to do some mighty deed,
Which would include all men in its effects,
And show a man's full power unto men.
That dream I had so very long ago,
When I seemed standing by the loud sea's shore
And a soft, subtle voice, not like mine own
Nor issuing from the heavy lips, and yet
Pulse-driven from the vocal heart, did flow
Away from me unlessening, until,
On-swelling to most distant worlds, it drew
Sweet answers from them ;—was it then, I ask
But the mere phantom of night-feeble eyes?
Or rather of such stable elements,
And of such large extent as fronts unharmed
The full puissance of the waking life?
Where'er this purpose had its secret rise,
It now is stablished on each sovereign peak
And prominence of strong material life,
With bed-rock of experience underneath.
I find each man is likened unto all,
And dare not doubt but that there is a way
For each to send impression of himself
Unto the rest.   And therefore have I made
Long search among the mystic agencies
Which, widely scattered and unused, weigh down
The glimmering floors of inner consciousness,
For hint of that,—the universal voice—
The universal deed, which I required.

Again, for long hours have I, anxious, sat
Beside the gate of the Unseen, with none
Save those twin-sisters who its warders are,
Silence and Solitude, for company :
While they would cast upon my quiet heart
Their shadows lined with light etherial,
And, with a world-oblivious touch, would close
Each open pore and earth-stained aperture
Which might leak excellence ; but all in vain :
For I was still unhelped in my design.
Then I have passed long time 'mongst men to watch,
In stealth, their meetings and voice-interchange,
Habits of speech and speech's accidents,
Contact of common word, or the blind touch
Of unaccustomed rage ; for some dim sign
Of that self-ligature which leashed their thought
Unto an aim so near, or that repulse
Of counteracting wills which stifled it ;
But nothing have I gained save strength of hope.
And though I still can speak but brokenly,
Or act but weakly as the others do,
Yet have I found it good to make the search.

AGAINST THE WIND.

Hear the wind blow !
    Let it go,
    Bearing rain,
    Bearing snow,
    Loss or gain :
    Never chase it !
    Only face it !
      Cry, hollo !

Seek for its source !
Measure its force !
    It can tear
    From thy hold,
    But the bare,
    And the old.
    Still thou hast
    What is best :—
      Never care !

Behind is but drift ;
Before a rich gift :
    Haste along !
Though breathless the pace,

There is breath for a song !
There is heart for a race !
   Quicker meet
   The new sweet,
    Or the wrong !

How flies from the mind
What maketh one blind !
   From the heart,
   The causes of fear !
   A fresh start !
Now the end is so near.
   Gods invite
   Whom they smite ;—
    Give a cheer !

A PRAYER TO MORNING.

Morning, sole fugitive of earth's First Day,
  Who dwellest still in the Beginning,
Between the light and darkness hid away—
  Pursuit but feints and flushes winning—
A simple boon I ask, in simple lay ;—
  Waken not all who now in slumber lie,
  But spare thou some, and, Morning pass them by.

What is the charm wherewith thou wakest man?
  Drain'st thou the stars to water his dry heart !
Or do thine eyes which sunsets never scan,
  By simply bidding, make the night depart?
Whate'er thy power is, be this thy plan ;—
  Search thou all hearts while yet in sleep they lie,
  If some are still aweary, pass them by.

Sleep hath so brief a time to work her will ;
  Grief works so fast, and hath such lengthened days ;
Though to the sorrows which the heart o'erfill
  Night saith ; "Ye are but phantoms, truant fays,
Come ! follow me unto my home's dark sill,"
  Yet shall some waking eyes burn as with lye ;
  Morning, in mercy, simply pass them by.

But there are some who, wakened, look so far,
  That day seems but a light spot at their feet ;
Whose hearts are bruised against the sunset's bar,
  And sleep is death unto some vision sweet,
And blots the hope of things which never are :—
  To such, a double gift do not deny,
  Or, Morning, show them grace and pass them by.

And, Morning, take thou heed ! there be a few
  Who find the flood of sleep a shallow stream ;
Whose souls are still erect as first they grew,
  And are not all submerged as others seem:
One such I know ; and, if thou dost not view
  Some spot awake whene'er thou drawest nigh,
  Then, Morning, weep and slowly pass me by.

THE MODEL.

See, how the light refines itself upon her !
As her diffusive beauties fill the air :
How golden faeries gather in her honor,
   And make a circle round her charmèd chair !
      That, as she chastely sits,
      No evil thing that flits
      Shall come anigh her there.

Unlike to thought is her long revery :
   And yet there may about her cling
Some touch of Thought's last poise and spring
   Upon his dusty boundary,
   Which lightly sways her now—
   A land-breeze blowing her to sea—
      While on her peaceful brow,
The growing glory of supernal scenes
      Slow supervenes.

Think not that they who purely trust
   The eager vision of the universe,
See not beyond the eye of lust ;
   Nor know, before they swift disperse,

The forms of free-winged purities,
　　　Which flutter, shadow-wise,
　　　Round secret-holding eyes,
Concealing all their ecstasies.
　　Nay! they shall win in faery races,
　　And snatch the veils from angel faces,
　　　Nor anywhere be blind :
　For eyes not bent in backward glances,
A forward force of seeing find,
　Which, past the common, still advances
Into the land where sight is unconfined :
　Where holiest truths are ever common,
　　　And sweet scenes summon.

　　Doth now she see or dream?
　　　From which side of the soul
　　　Do these scenes roll?
　　　For it doth seem,
That as a babe upon her mother's breast
　She lies in infantile content ;
　　And for her nourishment—
　　As beauty's holy eucharist—
That mother passes back and forth her hand,
　And wondrous pictures in her sight do stand :
　　And while she still is seeing,
　　The sight grows into being
Till she is twin with her who feeds :
　And, sisterly, they wander now at will

In glorious meads ;
Pass groves whose coolness has no damp or chill,
  And streams whose waters do so smoothly glide,
That images that fall there e'er abide.
  But in her heart a silent sorrow grew,
Because, among the radiant beings there,
  Some did not look on her, nor knew
Her presence, nor, with what despair,
  Her heart did beat her beauty in their faces,
Or fling before their feet her newest graces;
  Till near she seemed to death ;
When her companion said unto her : "See !"
  And far away she saw, with bated breath,
One coming towards her potently :
  A glorious mien he had, and, o'er his head,
A star blazed which illumed his way ;
  And coming straight to her he calmly said :
"I see thee as thou *art*, and, from this day,
  Thou art mine own and shall be seen of all,
Since thou art seen by Love who is perpetual."

    Surely she did dream ;
For now the joyous painter comes to her,
  Holding a canvas whereon naught doth err,
    And all her beauties beam :
    "Waken thou perfect one,"
    He said, "the work is done :
        See !
    I have painted thee."

AN ARROWHEAD.

Sole relic of a race which once was here,
   And broke earth's olden solitudes before
A gentler people gained her friendly ear ;
   With lengthened histories art thou written o'er—
Thou who wert wrought to bear in flinty text
   A passioned moment's keen and forceful score—
With what hast thou death's dusky hollows vexed,
     That back upon the summits of the world
     These ghostly shapes are numerously hurled !

O wild, first children of earth's ecstasies !
   Brood of a bird who built her nest in storms ;
Whose lullabies were roared from off the seas,
   Or thunder-dropped from tempests to the arms
Of boisterous spirits neighboring in woods :
   The thought of you old Nature's heart new-warms,
And calls her from those calm and silent moods,
     Wherein, with finer forces, she doth now create
     The modern man who knows to conquer hate.

Where hast thou lain concealed these hundred years,
   Dark piece of flint? who bent the bidding bow

Which sent thee forth—guide of a flock of fears?
  Perhaps some fiery youth but made a show
Of his new prowess ; or some chieftain hoar
  His wild rage loosened thus against his foe,
Who bore thee in his heart to Pluto's shore,
         And, with a bow
   Slow-builded from a century's arc of pain,
  Sends his kept hate back upon the earth again.

PEACE IS BUT WEAKNESS OF SPIRIT.

Peace is but weakness of spirit ;
 Rest but the sleep of decision ;
Sleep but a death-fall or near it,—
 Divinities' scorn and derision.

Is all your desire conceded
 By the powers of giving and keeping?
Your longing never impeded?—
 A road to be traversed with leaping?

Build thou thy bed at its ending,
 On the further side of denying ;
Rest *there*, and gods while attending,
 Shall guard and hallow thy lying.

MORNING SONG.

Wake ! wake, my dreamer, wake !
Let Sleep no longer slake
  His thirst in thy full heart,
  But, satisfied, depart,
    For my lips' sake ;
    Wake ! Wake !

Rise ! rise ! the day is near !
Long since, each crimson pier
  Was built for her pure arch ;—
  List ! hearest thou not the march
    Below the skies ?
    Rise ! Rise !

O let the Day's swift race
Begin from thy pure face !
  And let that be her goal,
  To make my gladness whole !
    No minute waste !
    Haste ! Haste !

THE BRIDEGROOM.

Here I sit, locked safe in my room again !
　　How well I have fooled them, priest, Jack and 'Light !
By the seat in the elm and the uncloaked pane,
　　Was I truly as one at the rite ;
'Though I marvel to think I endured the strain.

She is mine and not his by Love's own law,
　　Since her joy would last if she came to me.
'Though for me she thinks she cares not a straw,
　　Her eyes are so veiled that she may not see
'The right of my claim and his false title's flaw.

But I've married her fast in spite of them all ;
　　Each promise I made ere his slow tongue spoke ;
And ere he had slipped on her finger small
　　The circlet of gold, with a mystic yoke,
I had girded her spirit beyond recall.

And a husband's faith I will keep with her,
　　'Though another roof is above her head ;—
From my chair this night I will never stir,
　　Lest if once I should lie on my brideless bed
Hot tears those magic espousals should blur.

So here will I sit and transmute, till the sun,
Love's common modes to immortal ways ;
To-night must this magical work be done ;
For to-morrow then and all her future days.
Her perfect soul by such arts shall be won.

Let him have her at night then, if he will,
When her eyes are closed and her spirit dull ;
For the days she is mine, when life doth thrill
Her lids apart, and her heart is full
Of delights which the brutal night shall spill.

The time shall come, aye ! it soon shall be here,
When the subtle bond to her heart is known,
And the truths of Love shall indeed appear ;—
She may dream some night that she sees her *own*,
And shall wake o'er *Jack's* strange face with fear.

Or if not so soon from her heart is cast
The dusk which divideth its white and red,
Yet when Death shall call to her, going past.
Though Jack shall be standing close to her bed,
As she goes, my face will she look upon *last*.

THE LOST FLOWER.

I cannot say how first I knew
    Of that lost flower ;
Whether old legend left some clue,
    In childish hour,
    Which I have followed as I grew ;
Or other flowers of some great loss
Have whispered e'en mine ear across ;—
Yet well I know that once was snatched
From earthly fields a flower unmatched.

And I have heard or dreamed or guessed
    It thus befell.
That of all flowers the first, the best
    Of field or dell,
    Was borne from reach of human quest ;—
A mighty prayer which once was prayed,
Like that by Laodamia made,
Wrought this great marvel o'er the earth
And dimmed for after times its worth.

A woman by her husband's tomb,
    In ceaseless grief,
So sent her longing through the gloom,

So sought relief,
That all the flowers then in bloom
Did, sorrowing, with her kneel,
And urged her iterate appeal;—
"Send him not back along the skies,
But give one word from Paradise."

The gods were moved, but first demand—
    Despite their cries—
The fairest member of their band,
    For sacrifice ;
And they turned not that dread command.
Thus was there taken, for all time,
The sweetest flower of purest clime,
To be translated to a word
Which by one soul alone was heard.

A HOMELY FACE.

A homely face I sometimes meet—
A woman's face that should be sweet;
Pain's spectral hand doth touch my heart,
And vague tones from its hollows start,
As I pass by, with swifter feet,
The homely face that should be sweet.

Darkly I feel, as down the street
Some fairer face I chance to meet,
That highest wrong was somewhere done,
Upon that hapless, passing one
(A wrong that 'gainst the soul doth beat),
Which homely made what should be sweet.

The hand divine knows no defeat,
And still doth fashion all things meet:
But what most fair it doth create,
Is set within an earthly state,
Where beauty e'er must beauty greet,
If fair shall last what should be sweet.

The face starts fair; but if it meet
With life's coarse forms 'twill them repeat;
And loathsome labor, sordid aim,
And hateful touch of deeds of shame,
Shall make and mould with cunning fleet,
The homely face that should be sweet.

THE LEADER.

Through toilsome ways the host moved on in might :
  The sun looked not upon their camp ; before
His thinnest wedge was slipped between the night
  And their dream-laden hearts, they had once more,

With their own force, the mighty burden raised,
  And set fresh foot upon some dusky steep :
So late they rested, evening was amazed,
  And darkness wearied, waiting so for sleep.

Sometimes the query ran along the line
  "Where is the enemy? doth he wait or run?"
But when the leader heard he made no sign
  Still only gave the stern command "March on !"

But nightly when the weary soldiers slept,
  Mysterious councils sat within his tent :
The silent courier to his presence crept,
  And ere the dawn was on new missions bent.

At last, upon a plain most opportune—
  What time the Day, in childish revery,
Her sweets doth balance o'er the knee of Noon—
  The leader set his men for final victory.

" Behold the foe," he said, while from afar
  Came sounds of singing and salutes of friends,
And soon a host like to themselves drew near,
  And every man a friendly hand extends.

Again the leader spoke, and on his face
  Benignant smiles built garrisons of peace,
And old command was blent with newer grace ;
  And with his words all lingering murmurs cease.

"A short march leadeth he who finds a foe
  For man in man : there is but one long course ;
It lies the way that all mankind must go:—
  Up ! and away again with double force."

THE PERMANENT.

What thing shall last?---
The tree that slowly mounts in light,
Till the span of a thousand years it shows,
And grasps from the last hour's blazing height
Some prize it saw when it first arose ;
More swiftly goes ;—
It shall not last.

What thing shall last?—
Temples and monuments of eld,
Symbols of faith both in gods and men,
Have fallen and gone with the names they held,
And perfidy wanders where they have been ;
Now darkens Then ;—
These did not last.

What thing shall last?—
Tempered in flame and sure of seat
And his granite brow in scorn left bare,
The mountain waits ; but there shall beat
Time's change-sharp moments, and shall wear
It past repair ;—
That shall not last.

What thing shall last?—
A sacred gift that one day rose
From the soul I loved, when my love was told ;
A smile? a look? Let him name it who knows,
But it blent with my being, and behold !
Grows never old ;—
This thing shall last.

THE VEIL.

I saw the bride in her veil ;
   (Where now is the bride?)
Yet was not hid that face love-pale,
Where timid smiles did full and fail.
   (Where now is the bride?)

I saw the veil on the bride :
   (Where now is the veil?)
A woman sitteth weary-eyed.
With face love-bare and heart denied.
   (Where now is the veil?)

THE SOUTH WINDS.

From the centre of the year,
From the sun-warmed heart of growth ;
From the toil of its beat anear,
The weary winds come loth ;—
Having no rest from their year-long labors,
Nor any release from their fragrant loads,
String-voiced with a murmur of tabors
Caught in the long, slow forest roads :
Down-drooping with moisture, smitten with song,
Come they northward along.

From the depths of life they spring ;
From the lips of spring as breath ;
From the lord of earth their king,
Words of toil they bring and a wreath ;
For toil is constant where they come from,
But Nature's toil, not man's, I mean ;
Since often man has an idle palm
When Nature herself is busiest seen ;
For Nature and Sloth seem there in league.
And Nature's toil is man's fatigue.

But Nature wearies towards the North ;
　The weary winds, with faltering feet,
Come and draw the white cloth forth
　From the workman's task still incomplete ;—
They call to the workman, "Renew thy strokes !"
　While the streams in pity cry back " Hush ! "
And trees behind their masking cloaks,
　Grow mute before the wild-birds gush ;—
Man's sole reply is a sound of tools ;
　His sad heart owns that Labor rules.

THE BLIND BIRD.

A strange thing happened to me one day,
As I walked afield in the early May;
 I saw a bird all in crimson and black,
 Who followed with ease a white bird's track,
While the white bird sang as though leading the way.

The second bird, all in crimson and black,
Had no song of his own as he followed the track,
 But often some strain of the sweet, singing guide
 He repeated with awe, in a gentle aside,
As the tuneful strokes of his wings grew slack.

But just as he passed, all in crimson and black,
Fatigued, to the ground he fell downward, alack !
 In my hand I took him, with piteous mind,
 And lo ! I beheld that my fair bird was blind ;—-
My bird who had followed the white bird's track.

SONG.

When hand doth touch a hand,
　Two lives may greet ;
When folded lips expand
Like flowers in the sand,
　Upon the brows retreat ;
　Some words are meet.

Upon the fertile cheek,
　Beneath the eye's fine heat,
Lips sparkle as they speak,
　And tremble and intreat
　For place more sweet.

When lips to lips make four,
　Speech folds her wings ;
And Music, hovering o'er,
　With rapture sings.

LAMENT.

Oh, what is the earth's endeavor,
   That it's work is yearly repeated?
And what is man's, that forever
   The work of his hands is defeated ;
And the goal he strives to attain
Must be reached again and again?

O Labor, O cruelest Master !
   Why sendest thy angels of wasting—
Thy agents of woe and disaster—
   Corrupting the fruit at the tasting ;
And setting a term to the plants of the field,
And weaving ruin with all that they yield?

MISGIVINGS.

Like parting lovers
  Thy lips part;
Like gentle rovers
  Loth to start.
By breath of passion
  Never curled;
In thoughtful fashion
  Often furled.
If kisses find them,
  Like a breeze,
Shall they unwind them,
  If they please?
Or further bind them
  In their ease?
If from their sleeping
  They are stirred,
Does't follow weeping
  Shall be heard?
If love doth sever
  Lips peace-locked,
By sighs and fever
  Are they rocked?—
Shall it be mine
  To trouble thine?

AN APOLOGUE.

The seer gave unto the suppliant
  A tender plant having a double root :
Blessed him as was his righteous wont,
  And said, "Plant well, and great shall be the fruit."

The seeker's prayer had been for happiness ;
  This gift the sole response the seer made ;
But since, 'twas said, he did all joys possess,
  The suppliant was glad that he had prayed.

Then he departed thankful to his home,
  And crossed his fields and found a lonely spot,
Where richest herbage showed the fertile loam,
  There set his plant most carefully I wot.

With stealthy frequency he sought the place,
  To watch the plantlet's steady growth ;
But none he told ; he would its ripening grace
  For him alone—to pluck and feast on both.

A wondrous growth the curious plant revealed,
  And soon became a great and shapely tree ;—
So great, he feared it could not be concealed,
  And some one else its fairy fruit might see.

As if in answer to his strong desire,
  Some spectral blossoms to its foliage came ;
They seemed like shadows of some inner fire
  That could not waken into living flame.

These quickly faded, and no fruit appeared ;
  The foiled leaves fell and empty branches died ;
The man grew sick, as with a fever seared,
  To whom all cooling water was denied.

At last, in his distress, he sought the sage,
  And told him what had happened to the tree ;
Hoping the wise one would his pain assuage,
  By giving him some magic remedy.

"O fool !" the sage responded to his suit ;
  "The plant I gave thee was a border plant ;
'Plant *well*,' I said, 'and great shall be the fruit' ;
  But thou hast planted *ill* and all fruit want.

Thou shouldst have set it by thy *neighbor's* bounds ;
  Its double root asked food of double field ;
It would not make the seasons' weary rounds
  Unless some fruit it might thy *neighbor* yield."

NO BEAUTY THERE.

Is there a place where darkness doth not lay
Her dewy mesh to snare the earliest ray?—
Where plants stand ever bare of that swift-fruit,
      Which needs no aid
      Of petal-spade
      About its root?—
    Then may one say and swear
    That Beauty was not there,
    If he would hope to shirk
    All blame for his poor work ;
      That earth was bare
      Of all things fair,
    Where he lived lone with care.

Hath earth some hollow where the air-streams fail
And perish, that the flowers spread no sail ;
      Until a vampire mould
      Consumes the fruity freight
      Stored in each fragrant hold?
      Whoever liveth there
      May say and swear
      "It was my doom
    To see no flowers bloom
      Upon the air.

If one hath never seen a fair girl's eyes
Burning love-beacons, till the red waves rise
       To put such fires out ;
    Nor stooped some tender words to hear,
    And stilled his heart for very fear
    Its beat would put them all to rout ;—
    Why, he may urge the weak excuse,
    "There's nothing lovely for my use ;
      How could I work or rhyme
      In such a clime ?"

Is there a sky where clouds shall never sprall
    In sunlight's dreamy thrall,
  On seamless, easy floors ?
      Nor wake to float
      In lucid rote,
  Aflush with the joy that soars ?—
      Then let one loudly cry,
      "Pardon each idle year ;
      Art will not flourish here,
      And here live I."

Is there a land where eyes can never close
Except in sleep, and sleep bring no repose ?
Where the large spirit which the day has filled,
    Has all the flying views
    Which entered at those spiral avenues,
      By darkness spilled

Ere they have rested wing?—
"Then let one say for doing nought,
I have lived there and life has taught
No song to sing."

Perhaps there be some house of sob or sigh,
The shrinking stars will not pass by ;
    Or pass refusing
      Their clairvoyant musing,
And their holy attributes?—
If thou dost dwell in such,
    O silent, heavy one,
    Was there not still the sun,
Of slender, pleasant touch?

Or dost thou grope where the communion light—
The universal speech of all things bright—
Tells not the river what the heavens say :
Tells not each tree his brother's history,
With quiet voice and sweet prolixity,
Nor carries subtle greetings far away ;—
Then mayst thou lack the poet's speech,
    And truthfully declare,
      "Oh ! there was nothing fair
      Within my reach."

Or hast thou always dwelt in caves,
Where day about the threshold raves

To thy mad ears ;

Until the flowers that round her gleam
As only Nature's frothings seem,
Through thy false tears?—

Then mayst thou say and swear,
That Beauty was not there ;
And thou shalt find excuse
For all of song's disuse,
If on thy darkened walls
Her shadow never falls.

SONNETS.

TO H. M. A.

Friend of my need ! I have not seen thy face ;
  Yet distance hath not power to wholly hide
  What man thou seemest where thou dost abide.
Strange things are done within the deeps of space :
Swift carriers run there, bearing every grace
  Which ever shone from man beatified :
  Rare mirrors are there set across which glide
The shadowy figures of a perfect race.

Friend of my heart ! with thee I have not met ;
  Yet through the day, thy name to me can bring
Such visions of old saints, mine eyes grow wet :
  But in the eve, it doth a better thing :
For then it seems the green branch of a tree
Which night shall dew with dear expectancy.

TO J. E. L.

Disease, that, like a curious child, doth break
  The pebbles of our lives, hath broken thine :
  And hath beheld the white-faced fragments shine,
Benignant in the light of God, and take
Immortal beauties for the fracture's sake :
  As broken heavens of night their stars resign,
  Which through the day's completeness make no sign.
But rare the blow which shall such glories make,
Though blows should shatter every life that lies
  Upon the narrow beaches of this world;——
Oh ! I would rather give to some glad eyes,
  One moment of thy gleaming, then be hurled
Back to the ocean of eternal fullness,
Than live, a rayless whole of polished dullness !

THE RUNNER.

(DIED JANUARY 21ST, 1884.)

O wait, fleet runner of the unseen track,
  With snowy feet unsoiled by what they smite
  So lightly in their exquisite, pure flight !
Wait for me only, till I learn the knack
Of running freely at thy swallow back !
  For I am breathless, tired, and mine eyes
  Are so unused, dear one, to these bright skies.
Temper thy speed, that I may never lack
Thy footfall's singing sound ; nor fail at last,
  To have my heart beat so responsively,
  That mine own feet may feel the ecstasy
Of thine ; then fly thou slow or fly thou fast,
  I shall o'ertake thee, though I fall asleep ;
  I shall o'ertake thee early, though I creep.

OLD NEW-YEAR'S DAY.

Pale, patient day ! I doff the hat to thee,
In pity of thy mute unnoticed woe.
Who, seeing thee so humbled and so low,
Thinks of the time when thou, sweet deputy,
Stoodst forth alone the New Year first to see
    And serve, as she unwound her veil of snow,
    Flushing in all the Christmas afterglow,
And glad of face, beheld humanity?

Now when for twelve days she hath moved along
    The common paths of earth, hath seen joy die,
    Love lessen, wrath arise and dim the sky,
And with her gift of life, men doing wrong :
    In mourning garb, grief-drawn and tear-grimed face,
    She first meets thee and asks thy pity's grace.

BRAZIL.

No longer is there doubt ! no more disguise !
  Thou who wert lurking in the distant shade,
  Watching a farce by royal spectres played
On rotten boards of coffined monarchies,
Com'st forth at last with mirth about thine eyes,
  The true Brazil, a fair and noble maid,
  Who with the people laughed, with them delayed,
To show the true way of Democracies.

Men ask "Shall she abide?" Nay ! is there need
  Of blood and tears to charm thee to the land?
  Or shall the people loathe a stainless hand?
Sooner than that ye twain shall part—take heed—
  Shall fires drink up again their blackest smoke !
  Or tumult mend all dreams it ever broke !

THE TAKING TESTS THE SONG.

If one would learn the worth of his own song,
  Its formal beauty and essential might ;
  Or would behold with consecrated sight,
Its place of issue and the holy throng
Which still unto that pure abode belong ;
  Let him unlock, with some soft, minor key,
  That chamber of his voice where his heart be,
And mingling with its store the frequent, broad dipthong
Of tender chords as sole accompaniment ;
  Go sing to one song-deaf from very birth
  The sorrow which constrains him or the mirth,
Until their spirits are sufficient blent ;—
  Let him look after at the deaf one's face ;
  If that is stirred, his song hath, surely, grace.

OPPOSED.

Two hapless spirits were as east and west,
  Where, like opposing stars brightening their darts,
  They sent the passion of their scornful hearts
Across the careless earth, peace-lover blest,
Stationed between and mightily at rest.
  O Hate, why doth thy dumb immensity
  Divide so soon the souls that angry be?
Why must it be so far from breast to breast,
When their opposing beats give a recoil?
  Why may no power but Pain swim the abyss?—
Ah! if the sound our tears make when they fall
  Might cross, or sighs repentant lips dismiss
Be ferried, somehow, to the other shore;
Who knows, but souls themselves might soon pass o'er?

MIDSUMMER. ·

This is the balance of all growing things ;
   And Nature now inspects her yellow scales
   Poised upon silence, and secure from gales :
Against man's toil and care there fairly swings
The equal value of his harvestings,
   In perfect plain of equal counter-weight ;
   As East and West when skies immaculate
Unclasp each heavy cloud that to them clings.

The mute alarms of Nature's noting cease ;
   She doth remember all the spring-time songs
Which freely fell, and counteth their increase ;——
   The scale dips gently to the heart that longs,
Loaded with autumn's overplus of cheer,
With hopes fulfilled, heart-calms and courage clear.

BETWEEN THE EARTH AND SUN.

I.

How many wondrous things, O sun ! have flown
  Between the earth and thee, this ample day !
  How since the morn hast thou diverged away
From earth, and tracked the morning stars alone,
To let them through ! At first, to me was blown,
  As yet upon my bed I listening lay,
A sound of barriers broken musically,
And living streams that flowed in rapturous tone
Over the shattered bars.   Before mine eyes
  Passed breathless birds with furtive signs,
  The clouds that cloaked their gradual designs
And airy marvels from o'erladen skies ;
  While oft I heard the whispering, unseen throng,
  Whose robes left fragrance as they passed along.

BETWEEN THE EARTH AND SUN.

II.

O sun and earth ! the spaces that divide
Your shores are full of radiant voyagers,
Heaven-deserters and star-frequenters:
The glories that upon your breasts abide,
Are but the wreckage of that sacred tide—
Shreds from the garments of that crowded line ;
The light is but their banner's beauteous shine ;
The winds but answer to their onward glide ;
The varied hues that hourly fall and fade,
Are only flashings of their searching eyne ;
And heat the force they cannot all confine,
Since in their hearts a boundless force is laid ;
Music is echo of their onward flow,
And love, the subtle, deathless undertow.

MY SONGSTRESS.

I cannot love those birds of shallow song
And painful consciousness, that perch aloft,
And lightly, since the sun is warm, the air is soft,
Rehearse some common melody so long,
The sleep-curled ear heeds not the noisy throng
  That beat its cloistered ways with pebbly feet :
  I hate those birds of taut, bow-string conceit,
Who force afar, alike on weak and strong,
Their sharpened strains ; but I love well the one
  Who broodeth mutely in the impatient air,
  Bridging all space with silence, till most fair,
Immortal songs get mingled with her own ;
  Then flies away to some dark cypress bower,
  And softly sings as one who counts her store.

LOVE'S RETROSPECT.

I

When first I walked before thy strange abode,
  I marvel if the hollow of thy hand did not
  Appall thee, with a knowledge then begot,
Of sudden emptiness that seemed a load ;
Or yet if like a many stranded goad,
  The fingers did not meet the stricken palms,
  And lips then startled from their thoughtless calms,
With keen presentiment of another mode,
Rend suddenly the fabric of a smile
  Hung from their arches.   Faileth every sign,
  Found in the earthly, seen in the divine,
If then the runnels of thy heart, so smooth erewhile,
  Paused not acutely, at a spasm's stroke,
  As if with double currents they did choke.

LOVE'S RETROSPECT.

II

It leads to wondering that no wood or stone
  Foretold my fortune to me ; that no token
  Was from the front of that swift rapture broken,
And by some swifter wind to my heart blown ;
That its dull reaches moved not for the coming one,
  Like boughs that quiver at the leaping song,
  As the bird singer flies with joy along
To perch thereon ; that love and love alone,
Lacks visible beginning, hath no bud
  Upon the stalk of change, but comes to all
  In primal perfectness ; that each may call
This vital wonder from his pregnant blood,
  And no convulsions rend him bodily,
  To give it room and progress to reality.

TO A NOBLE WOMAN.

I

Goodness, dear lady, which flows often dim
　Through subterranean ways of other lives,
　Springs to the light and pure refreshment gives
In thee.　But how may I that goodness limn?
Since force of Springs by accidental rim
　Is measured not, how fair soe'er it be,
　But by the clouds which gather from the sea
Its airy globes to strew with fingers slim
Upon the careful sieve of earth.　As long
　As seas shall toss upon their wakeful beds,
　And clouds shall watch beside their storm-swathed
　　heads,
To take from open hands—no longer strong—
　Escaping treasures ; shall thy good endure,
　Unmixed with brackish taste, or stain impure.

TO A NOBLE WOMAN.

II

As far as music strays beyond its instrument,
  Or heat beyond the boundaries of flame ;
  As far as wrong out-runs dim-sighted blame,
Or fragrance springeth past the pure extent
Of flowers still closed, nor make the slightest rent
  In their scarce-wove apparelings of light,
  Or far as beauties stretch beyond the sight ;—
So far, upon the pinions of a pure intent,
Thy goodness doth project its subtle force,
  Beyond the compass of the living fact ;—
  Breaks from the word, out-runneth e'en the act,
O'ertaking too the smile upon its course ;
  And meets with nought which shall not swift obey,
  Because in thine own heart obedience lay.

TO A NOBLE WOMAN.

III

Kindness enfolds thy spirit's gracious form,
 As heaven's blue transparency a star ;
 No drop of acid shall such fabric mar,
Nor shall it ever come to any harm
From beak of flame or talons of the storm ;
 And Hate shall throw her vitriol at thy face
 And make no scar ; for to thy lofty place
Cometh no hurt nor even vague alarm :
Secure thou restest where no foes impugn,
 Like some fair, foam-like cloud, beheld at even,
 Alone, far up the ample beach of heaven—
There where the sun did meet the fatal noon—
 To show supremely to our upturned eyes,
 How high the lucid tides of day did rise.

WHITE CLOVER.

Ah ! prim, pale sisters, so erect beside
    Your ruddy brothers lounging lazily !
    What holds you ever in that upright way ?
Has Fear's white sceptre brushed your forms and dried
The stream of motion wholly at flood-tide !
    But Fear, the leaper, never left your calms ;
    The scattered realms he rules with palsied palms,
But in the crevices of Courage bide,
And they are far apart.   Nor does it seem
    That Prayer who strains on tip-toe for her gains,
    Could show your peaceful poverty of pains.
Methinks you went to pray, but that a dream
    Of maiden love displaced the prayerful mood,
    Tinted the cheek and eased the attitude.

SECOND CHILDHOOD.

Bees circle round unopened flowers, and seem
  To build new barriers about the old,
  The fairy dwellers there again to hold,
When sunlight's ransom doth their souls redeem,
And every curven rafter, board and beam
  Of their pure prisons, turneth to a door,—
  Their marble walls bend backward to a floor.
Thus we, approaching slow the life supreme,
Find sleep expanding only to a dream
  By the first rending of the walls of sense ;
  The full awaking and the sight immense
And last inspired touches to the theme :
  These follow when we cross the second line
  Where playful spirits throw their shadows fine.

LOVE SONNET.

How doth thy flute-toned spirit modify
   All utterances o'erstrained that disappear
   Within the rose-rimmed orifice of thine ear !
Ah, how I long that instrument to try !
And blow the sounds of my humanity
   Into that artery of perfect song
   So feelingly, no heart's recurrent thong
Be needed to give pulses or velocity.
For every tone should have its central heart
   Of passion and omnipotence of flight :
   Then would I learn to touch each key aright,
That there should issue forth but fair report
   Of regions dimmed for holy mysteries—
   For love, for music and mute ecstacies.

TO ———

———— — -

I

Thy worth adorneth my unworthiness,
  As flowers of loveliest dreams the steep
Environs of the dark abyss of sleep.
Thy love's bright lily, like a pure caress,
Floats on the waters of my life's distress,
  And by the thread of thy true womanhood
  Is holden to the firmament of good
Thereunder fixed ; whilst from its golden dress
The winds of hate but smooth each petaly fold.
  O ! sacred flower, that wastest so thy sheen,
  By ever-watchful heavens art thou seen,
And thought a star unrisen—unforetold,
  Whose august path, as yet unbuilt, shall rise
  From earth's low levels to the highest skies.

TO ——

——

II

The day that riseth from her troubled bed
  Whereby the Night hath watched, seems not the same
  That last eve fell there like a quivering flame ;
The sun himself an unfamiliar head
Each morning shows, and when the mists have fled,
  Doth mint for me new worlds by all my ways,
  Fresh stamped forever with his changing rays—
Wasting his wealth as heir to some sun dead—
  The song-birds lead each year an alien spring,
Singing strange music of some unknown master
  But never friendly recognition bring ;
But thou, O friend, in joy or in disaster,
  More steadfast art than birds or sun or day,
  And turnest an unchanging face alway.

TO ———

III

What, sayest thou, would my life be without thee?
  'Twould be the sun's ray falling dark and chill ;
  A summer night that would no dew distil,
Or summer morn with no bird melody ;
An East that might sleep on impassively,
  While passed the unfellowed sun her close-shut gate,
  In solemn splendor and impressive state :
A sea that should not feel eternally
A keelèd foot or Morning's flashing skirts
  Upon her vacant and appalling floors,
  Nor ever cast a wave upon her hungry shores ;
A world where love is deadly, kindness hurts ;
  Waters wherein the swan doth sink, the lily drown,
  And flowerless fields that look forever brown.

SLEEP'S STAINED GLASS.

This seems the spot I laid me down upon ;
There is the tree my eyes last idled with,
Awaiting sleep.   I think I must have dreamed.
O Sleep !   O wondrous silver coronal
Of the dark-faced Fatigue ! Away ! Away !
I would not wear the flashing circlet now,
For all the dreams that ever gemmed it when
It lightly lay on love's too-blessed head.
Thou dost reveal too palpably and clear
The weakness of this heart ;—too soon dost show
The deep, dark hollows pitting what I thought
The smooth and perfect sphere of Nature ;
And with the raillery of demoniac souls,
Dost point out all the rents which mar
The garment of that life I thought so whole.
What strange and throbbing sights I have beheld !
I would forget, but I am driven to recall.

It seems to me that I lay watching the slow sun
Arch his way downward mightily,
When, suddenly, a dusky vapor rose
And stood between us, and put slowly out

Huge, shapeless and unpitying hands, which seized
His slender rays and turned them back upon himself,
Until their whetted flame tips did consume
Him utterly ; and then the form dissolved,
And, dissipate in finest dust, arose
Towards the bare heavens, and did overspread
Them like a film ; and all the heavens shrank
As from the touch of drought.   Thereat the stars
Appeared, but all so changed I scarcely knew them :
And a new dread appalled me as I saw
Their unfamiliar shapes ; and I beheld
With awe that they no longer kept with fear
The sacred level of the sky, but they
Emerged and stood out boldly prominent ;
And they did seem like palms and through the wide,
Disparted branches, shaken by the swell
Of their own swift expansion, gleamed their fair,
Smooth, slender stalks, fast rooted in the deeps
Of the Invisible.

           Then suddenly
New energies burst violently forth
Around me everywhere ; the earth assumed
An altered motion and the trees, with cloven trunks
Out-spread like wings, flew past me like huge falcons.
My prostrate form was winnowed by the shocks
Of an impassioned longing to partake
The new delirium and pursue the fugitives.

The blood went through my heart like knotted ropes,
Flowing with strong, convulsive throbbings out
To the swelled finger tips ; and painfully
A drop oozed through the overstrained flesh
And fell upon the ground. There as I gazed
Upon it with dilated eyes, the bright,
Red globule grew, respondent to the growing sight,
And evenly, curve by curve, diffused itself
Far round me over the denuded earth,
Now smooth as glass ; till all was crimson stained.
And slowly, fine dark lines, like veins, appeared ;
And I then knew the mesh of all my life
Had been concealed in that red drop and lay
There awfully apparent ; and I closed
My eyes in terror ; and confusion like
A mist rose up within me and fulfilled
My total being ; and the icy hand
Of Fear moved through it and distilled it all
In tears, which forced my lids apart and fell
Most plenteously.

       But when I looked again,
The red had vanished, and, instead, there lay
A soft transparency upon the earth,
Plating it over with a foil of pearl ;
And looking down, far downward, through
The vault immeasurable, I plainly saw
The countless multitudes of all who had

Been born upon the rim of earth, had died,
And then been duly sepulchred within it ;
And all the distant phantoms ceased their weird,
Mysterious movements, and in unison,
Turned their wan faces towards me ; while a few
Raised baneful, beckoning fingers, which aroused
Such strong, convulsive struggles, such concussion
Of the eternal, elemental Noes
Within me, that I woke amid the din
Of vast explosions, loud, reverberant,
And found me lying here alive.

MEMORY.

A FRAGMENT.

Here let me rest within this quiet grove !
These trees, like belted soldiers, shall keep watch
Around me while I sleep. Oh, how this day's
Hard up-and-down of feet, has shaken out
All my crushed life's bright grains, through double sieves,
Upon the dusty road, leaving behind
But husky coats of bran to fill the shrine
Of sleep ! Oh, that a wind would rise, and blow
It all away ere I awake !

(Spirits appear over the head of the sleeper, and move
about in the performance of some mysterious function.)

FIRST SPIRIT.

He sleeps too long !
  He draws too near !
O sweetest singer of our throng,
  Go bend above his ear,
And sing an earth-remembered song
  Of love, to hold him here.

SECOND SPIRIT.

O great is the power of Sleep,
　And weary the toil of night !
Then only agile spirits weep ;
　For hands grow weary with solemn rite,
　From Sleep's broad door to keep the light,
　Where mortals lie with strainèd sight.

THIRD SPIRIT.

His eyes are beamless,
　But his sight is clear ;
His sleep is dreamless,
　And he comes so near.
O swiftest spirit of our train
Haste ! haste ! to the thronèd year ;
　And fall upon thy knees and cry,
"O back into his soul again
　Send awful Memory !"

Memory (approaching.)
I am the slow pursuer
　Of the rapid mind ;
I am the quick renewer
　Of the undefined,
Sweet image-lure,
　That flies to weave and wind,
　And backward bind
Eyes still impure.

(At the head of the sleeper)
O Sleep ! O umbrous clad !
  O slumber-masked and fire-centered !
In vain ! in vain thou lookest glad,
  For thou must lose what I have entered.
Dost not already hear the thrill
Of tensest wind and dangling rill,
  Within his heart?
Impassioned words of other days
And remnants of etherial lays,
  To his lips start?
In vain ! in vain ! thou dost embrace him,
While Memory's dappled favors grace him,
Disperse thy mists about his head !
  Retake thy kisses from his brow !
Behold ! the spirits all have fled.
  And I flee now.

Where was I when that gentle melody
Blew, like a breeze, across the forest of my thought,
And rustled so the dry, dropped leaves of fact,
That the bright birds of present ecstasies
Flew frightened from its branches? Oh, that I
Might find upon me the minutest clew !
How swiftly would I run to find that scene,
Which left this throbbing heart—this burning head !
But wheresoe'er it be, though near or far,
Right, left, or high or low, I doubt me not
My face is turned from it away. My thoughts

Lie in a draught that sucks them from the spot.
The present and the near are as the dead ;
Naught seems alive, except the past—the old:
Oh, I have drunk the liquor of some vine
Which trailed o'er graves ! or sipped the witches' wine
Of wild grapes born and nurtured upon ruins !
Or History doth wander here to muse,
And having found me as I lay asleep,
Hath plunged her withered hands within the vase
Of fresh, exuberant youth, and passed, by stealth,
Them dripping over my closed eyes, to wake
All aged and faded things to life, though age
And blight and death wrinkle the sapped Present.
My eyes are sunken in my head--so far
Contracted from their natural curves, they lie
Below the level of the living day ;
Yea ! on the bottom of the sea of vision ;
And see the many sights long fallen there.
But yet, there are no wrecks of olden scenes
Strewing the silent floor of these strange depths ;
Nothing is broken, ground or worn away,
By the soft serges of the upper stress
And beat of life ; all hath the same clear lines
As when the sharp, sure blades of my young sight
Carved them from Nature. Effortless and free,
My mind seems swimming in its first bright views:
And all have beauty printed on them plain,
Like the raised letters of the blind.

THE UNEQUAL LOVERS.

Hold thou thy life more firmly, careless one !
It leaves thy hand too lightly, and too oft
Doth play the truant to its sober nurse ;—
Sitteth without the threshold of its rest
Too often, in the eager sun of longing—
Hangeth on thy face, as ready, at a word,
To leap into mine own and perish there.
A little farther from me, dangerous girl !
Bind those strong, supple eyes or sit thou down
That they may sooner tire, from lifting up
Their glances.   Set those lawless hands to hold
Each other, lest their slender fingers braid
Themselves with mine ; and silence those small feet
Whose strokes upon the floor disclose the joints
Of my hard-wrought resolve, and penetrate
The feeble fabrication with their wedges.
Leave thy heart only free for this sad hour ;
Discharge its dangerous retinue of beauty ;
For hearts alone can grasp and strive with pain,
And I shall need thy young heart's help for mine.
      Thou art my ward ; and yet thy keeper needs
One key to guard thee safely from himself ;—

The key of thy dislike ; but thou dost wear
It out of sight, and leavest never closed
The doorway of my care, and in and out
Pass freely, laughing at my fears : yea ! oft
Will seat thee in the warder's room and smile
To see him try to fit his clumsy keys
Of sternness to the useless lock.
Did ever prisoner before so treat
Gruff jailor? or a bold offender turn
Sweet comrade of the offended in the act?
And yet thou sittest here, audacious one,
Secure and confident, in this close room
Of musty records, near the outer door
Which opens on the careless multitude,
And guardest it so fondly, that the dust
Doth settle on the latch. So thou, within
The violated chamber of my care,
Art free ; and I am captive of thy sweet,
Wild, wayward love. Alas ! what sacrifice,
That the bright folds of love, too soon unrolled
From thy fleet youthful heart, should ever float
Upon my ruined towers? But I must break
The weather-weakened cord of my mistake,
Which holds it, that it blow away, or like
A gauzy stream cast down from its high pinnacle
Through all the fine dissections of the air,
Be given back unto its elements.
Yes, dear delinquent, we have been too much

Together ; thy clear spirit has been stilled
Too often, in the hush of my calm thought ;
So that thy head bends ever o'er its pools,
To watch their pictured margins. Better far,
That the unfathomed floods of thy soft hair
Had drowned thy childish head in their pure deeps,
Than it should trickle down thy drooping form
And lie in little plashes on the floor.

And when I lift thee up and stroke thy head,
Drawing the scattered tresses back again
Within their natural channels, thou dost look
So calm and unsurprised at me, it seems
My dark, old form had bounded all thy visions.
But yet, I do believe implicitly,
That thou hast never seen me rightly, child ;
Thy looks have failed to reach me, being checked
By some swift after-thought of tenderness ;
Or the fine bow-curves of thine eager eyes
Have quivered in the grasp of the heart, and let
The loosened missiles fall upon the ground ;
Or some soft, early words of mine, not shrunk
And all misshapen by convention, must
Have taken form of thine imaginings,
And risen like a screen before me. Yes,
At most thou knowest my form and lineaments,
As one may know the letters of a word,
Which loosen not the meaning which they clasp.

Gray hairs do not affright you and you say,
" 'Tis but the underside of the leaf that turns
And brightens in the sun." Alas! my child,
The winds of death have grasped the hidden branches,
And do shake them threateningly. You smile each time
I speak of wrinkles, and with haste insist,
They are but "welcome crevices which show
The gleam and gold within." This hard dry hand
Would bruise thine own soft tender one,
Holding it rigid like an iron glove ;—
But you "would rub the metal till it shone
And showed your smiling, happy face in it" ; or kiss
The rugged thing and claim triumphantly,
That "lips were feebler, softer things than hands,
And yet the touch had never injured *them.*"
These arms that have been straightened and outstretched
Through many years of stiff expectancy,—
Could they be bended to the pliant curves
Which rounded youth might rest in easily?
Love would but warp their rigid muscles, girl ;—
Could never make them flexible again.
What, wilful, stubborn one, still unconvinced?
Still in your twilight blushes find the clue
To speech, and say, that you have seen my arms
"Cross over and enfold the spacious couch
Of the breast, and could they not, with lesser strain,
Meet midway and enclose one little sleeper?"
No, dear, fallacious reasoner, ever wrong !

For they would tremble all so fearfully,
That Sleep's veined onyx stones might soon be jarred
From thy smooth brow and fall upon the floor,
Breaking to frightful dreams ; then thou wouldst wake
And moan and welter in thy tears till day.

   The Years that build upon our upright lives
Their fatal stairs, until they reach the top,
And tear away the banner-breath with scorn,
Build ever on the front and openly ;
And thou mayst see that they have mounted high—
Already hang upon my breast, and make
Me bend a little towards them ;—pardon ! child,
This stoop doth bring thy lips so near mine own,
I could not help but kiss them. 'Twas the Years
I spoke of caused it.   But if thou couldst climb
With them, secure upon their frail supports,
Such kiss were not a theme for penitence.

   Too late, thou camest, little loiterer,
To build of fairy stuff the bridal room with me !
Thy fragile gems and dainty properties—
How will they match the strong well-chiseled stone,
Which I must lay with plumb-line in the walls?
How will thy careless, discontinuous touch,
Thy gleeful heapings of thy pretty toys
And handful throwings on the trembling pile,
Assist my steady cautious masonry?
But if the odd, unlovely structure rose,
Despite these sad discordancies of hand,

So high, it needed cover ; still the work
Must stop from graver difference ; for *I*
Could roof it only with the flat expanse
Of split, disjointed memories, through which
Oblivious rains would beat upon our heads;
But *thou* wouldst take the flawless, perfect piece
Of thine undamaged *present*, and wouldst dome
The room luxuriously. Besides, there is
The floor, my little, sweet incompetent;—
What wise, ingenious plan canst thou devise,
That we may jointly build the fitting floor?
For I am footsore, weary and worn out,
With treading on life's hard impossibilities,
Its sharp conventions and discomfitures,
And surging aspirations frozen stiff
In early ridges, by some merciless cold
Of quick heart-sickness, and so left to stand
Like awful corrugations in the brow of Doubt.
I have laid off my shoes and would acquaint
My feet with softer ways, where God doth not
So fend Himself with perils, wrap his truths
In hard ungracious obstacles, but leaves
The wondrous courses of His being all
Unclosed before us. Better shod art thou,
With wholesome energies which shield thy feet,
And strong enthusiasms ringing loud
Upon the flinty ways, and striking fire
Of fine exhilaration every step.

Why, thou mighst lay the floors with piercing thorns,
With upright needles or with adders' teeth,
And dance upon them painlessly ; nor think,
In thine invincible novitiate,
Which turns them into harmless, temperless blades
Of grass, what cruel, stubble fields they were
To my bare feet.

      But say 'tis all accomplished,
And we shut alone in that abode,
Wouldst thou not seek thine oriel window soon,
And stand there flinging forth thy voice with joy,
Feeding the doves of fancy with thy song,
And sketching faint thy morrows on the pane?
Whilst I beside my western casement, grave,
With ocean charts of yesterdays in hand,
Would sit instructing Death's black eagles there.
Too late, thou camest, O my torturer !
We both must travel many leagues before
We cross that width of bridal room and meet
With faces inward.   No despairing leap,
Nor violent clasping of unequal arms,
Could now reduce the space one little inch.   .

     How hath thy strange love grown, precocious reaper?
Can the waste fields of retrospect produce
Such golden fruitage? or the somber seeds
Of actualities so compensate
The gay, glad sower? But this is not love

You gather, child. Nay, hear me patiently ;
The seed of love is bright, like pearls, and hued
With sparkling joys ; and it is flung by Hope,
Far forward, as the sower sows, and sprouts
And blossoms as it falls ; but the hard grains
Thou scatterest were not taken from the keeps
And crystal treasuries of lavish youth,
But stolen from my granaries of sorrow.
Alas ! the fruit they yield has not the glow
And bloom of thine untarnished heart, but lies
In thy bright hand all staled by trembling touches,
Streaked by frequent tears, and withered by hot sighs.

But thou hast been too long here, fellow-heart ;
And now thou must go from me, for thy peace,
To places that await thee, noble tasks
That need thy little efforts, and to mirth
That may not float on any voice save thine :
And thou must hasten, ere the shining trail
Of one who goes before thee through this world,
Shall fade away ; already doth the shade
Of my hard rocks fall far along the way ;
And thy young eyes have turned so oft with mine
Upon the mighty outlines of my nearer goal,
They may not seize and bind the broken lines
And glimmering visibilities of thine.

Continue silent, child, and serious !
Letting my thought glide through thy thoughtfulness.

To reach the farthest turning-goal of doubt,
And come back freely to thy confidence.
　　Each age hath its own gifts and offices,
In fixed relation to the rest of life—
Man-life, or God-life, round it.　Child with child
Must join the margins of their separate joys,
Or leave the ragged edges so they wound.
Childhood alone doth have the sacred art
Of ministering to the child ;—holdeth the clue
To the near goods he needeth, or the power
To help him lift and fit them to his heart.
Youth only beat with youth can make the foil—
The precious writing sheet, whereon the heavens pen
Their holy formulas of happiness :
And man who strives alone with man, gains aught
Of God to demonstrate his victory.
Hear this ! the separate parallels of strands
Which make our song-life's noble instrument,
Do lack a crossing, vibrant warp to bind
The upper and the lower strings ; and thou,
So far away from me in thy tense youth,
Canst give but faint harmonic tones to-day
To my hard-smitten age so soon to break.

　　There is another meaning, earnest one,
In our fixed places here which touches, too,
Our places elsewhere ; for it seems
We measure here with careful, accurate hand

The flight we take hereafter from death's perch.
With life's first motions we draw slowly forth
From some dim, ductile mass of precious ore,
A golden thread, and wind unceasingly,
In even coils, and hold them on our arms :
Death but unwinds the thread and leaves us dizzy
Where it ends. So thou must run to work,
And draw with swiftness, till the gathered loops
Equal mine own ; for look thou at thine arm
So nearly empty,—all thou hast secured
Could scarcely serve thee for a wedding ring.

But when thou goest from me, I shall lose
Of precious things far more than I can count
Upon the failing finger-tips of speech.
My wondrous gains in thee have all been scored
Upon the luminous pages of thy presence :
Naught that's prepared for writing, is so broad
As that, or offers room, at best, for more
Than title page of name and arabesque of smile
For *finis* to it.   Absence hath no sage
Arithmetic to sum my losses by ;
And leaves me but a little book to print
Thy changeful image in.   Let me but read
Some first lines only of the wondrous volume,
Ere thou dost close it with thy parting look.

Here find I written with a trembling hand,
"The low, sweet song before the evening prayer ;"—

My prayer shall find less pleasing company
In sighs and groans. And here I find inscribed :
"The light which leadeth to my darkened room :"—
But I must grope my way there now alone ;
And here, "The airy bridge of dreams between
My morrow and my yesterday, o'er which
I draw, in calm, untroubled happiness,
The captive chain of all my past delights ;"—
Why, they must swim in floods of sleeplessness,
Or stay behind. But stay ! these literal forms
Are much too strong for my frail sight and break
The shafts of vision into vexing parts,
That, dropping, blind me with their rapid lights,
Leaving my brain confused. So let me close
The eyes to meditate, and read the rest
From the raised letters of thy vivid hand.
There ! that is better, child, and I proceed.
The hooks of thought we fling into the deep
Of unknown things, were long worn smooth with me,
And gathered nothing, when thou camest here
To barb them over with thy curious words,
And aid my feeble hand to draw them often forth,
To view the chance entanglements upon them.
But when thou goest from me, I shall walk
The turfless shore alone, and drag behind,
Through empty waters, those appendages,
Weary and praying for the rope of days
To drop apart, that I may fall and rest.

And there are beings who lie down with us at night,
Who slumber longer than the weary frame ;---
Spirits that fill the eye and move the hand,
And urge the heart into a quicker pace :
Eternal Beauty, Aspiration, Hope ;—
They will not waken at the harsh complaint
And heavy voice of age, obscurely heard,
Like the accustomed rumble of the street ;
But one must come and whisper tenderly,
Touching to motion the light wheels of the ear,
With the fine draft of music,—loading up
The spirit with the lure of morning ecstasy
And sweetest utterance, and quickening
The drowsy lids with silken whips of eyes
That play above them.

                    Thou shalt elsewhere be,
Some morning when I rise, alone, to meet
The day without these fairy ministrants.
I, who have stroked thy pleasant, loosened hair,
Until the hidden shuttle of the touch
Did weave its fluctuant flosses into cloth
Of floating gold, must grasp the slippery threads
Of incoherent energies to work
Them, somehow, into decent burial clothes.
These eyes that have so often lain at ease,
Within the peaceful Saturn-rings of thine,
To intercept thine own bright visionings,

Must early feel Death buckle up the lids
And press the lingering light out ruthlessly.

*　　*　　*　　*　　*

Thou weepest, but 'tis less from thine own pain
Than from thy sympathy with mine.
Ah, child, 'tis pleasing to dispute the point
With thee, and I am happy that to-day
Thou thinkest it is peace, to hold thy place
Of cramped and painful attitude and poise
Of labored equilibrium upon
The harsh projections of my shattered walls ;
But the relief of pliant muscles, ease
Of unstrained wishes and the liberal grace
Of natural actions led by aptitudes,
Shall safe receive thee in their gentle arms,
When thou dost loose thy hold about my neck,
And fall upon the lower, broader ground
Of youthful fellowship. There thou shalt find
Creatures with fine, smooth, tender hands like thine,
Whose clasp shall be love's sure cohesiveness,
Not the false holdings of my roughened ones
Which caught the fluttering fabric of thy youth
Upon their bramble touches. There thy feet
Shall don the holy shoon of pure Love's footprints,
As she guideth thee along the doubtful way
To perfect treasures stored for thee by Heaven,
In open coffers of supreme embraces,

Or beneath dark stones of sad experience.
But thou must never cease to follow her,
Nor ever fail to put thy willing feet
Exactly in the traces of her own,
Until thou gainest so the fashion of her step,
That the hard earth shall soften under thee.
And thou shalt set thy fingers only where
Love's cunning hand hath made a place for them,
And lined it with the blessing of her smile.
Yet fear to be too eager in pursuit,
Or play too fast thine mimicries ;
But follow leisurely the thoughtful way,
Leaving each object with a solemn joy,
And looking often back regretfully.
Be not afraid to rest, to lie thee down,
Aye, close the eyes and sleep ; thou shalt not lose
One line of progress in the longest dream ;
For love shall stoop and take thee in her arms
And carry thee till morning—harken ! child—
When thou mayst wake to find me bending over thee.
Yes, little weeper, thou shalt come again
To me, and I shall claim thee though my right
Be challenged by the highest Lords of Heaven.
Thou art mine own to-day ; shall one pretend
That there is law to void my ownership,
Until I waive my legal titles? What !
Because I send thee out to play an hour,
To scatter song and gather fragrancies ;

To stoop o'er dazzled, blinded flowers and make
The sunlight visible : to run beside
Some lonely stream to keep it company,
Or throw thy moving, pliant image on
The silent pools aweary with their fixed
Tenacious grasp of moveless shadows there ;—
Do I bestow thee on the natural world,
And thus abandon mine own equities?
No ! sweetest chattle of my heart's estate
And best possession of my future, No !
Thou dost remain mine own immortal property ;
Mine ! by the strong preemption of the soul ;
Mine ! by a clear, divine investiture ;
Mine ! by the desperate struggles of the mind
To break the barriers of the hands and lips,
And gain the perfect, interfusing touch
Of the full, liberal life of Heaven ; and mine !
By my supreme and sacred poverty
'Fore God and awful emptiness of hand.
Though all the Hierarchs of Heaven stand
Opposing, and God's august magistrates
Lend their commissions to the infamy,
I would protest against the deed so forcibly,
And make such clamor at the false decree,
That holy angels should grow pale in fear—
Should fall upon their knees and pray in whispers.

Go now, my child, contend with weaker hearts
Than mine, in love and loving exercise ;

Strengthen thyself with thought, and teach thine eyes
To find the weakness of thine adversary's ;
Constrain thy spirit to a dart and hurl
The missile 'gainst the thickened rind of the world
And break it open ; tutor thy weak hands
Till iron seemeth soft and thou canst twist
The lightnings round thy fingers, like a curl
Of thy bright hair ;—then come again to me,
And we shall make a pair whom God is proud of.

www.ingramcontent.com/pod-product-compliance
Lightning Source LLC
Chambersburg PA
CBHW030824270326
41928CB00007B/891